Sir Philip Sidney
and *Arcadia*

Sir Philip Sidney and *Arcadia*

Joan Rees

Rutherford ● Madison ● Teaneck
Fairleigh Dickinson University Press
London and Toronto: Associated University Presses

Associated University Presses
440 Forsgate Drive
Cranbury, NJ 08512

823
S56 zr

Associated University Presses
25 Sicilian Avenue
London WC1A 2QH, England

Associated University Presses
P.O. Box 39, Clarkson Pstl. Stn.
Mississauga, Ontario,
L5J 3X9 Canada

Library of Congress Cataloging-in-Publication Data

Rees, Joan, 1923–
    Sir Philip Sidney and Arcadia / Joan Rees.
        p.   cm.
    Includes bibliographical references (p.   ) and index.
    ISBN 0-8386-3406-0 (alk. paper)
    1. Sidney, Philip, Sir, 1554–1586.   Arcadia.   I. Title.
PR2342.A6R38   1991
823'.3—dc20   89-46411
                                                            CIP

PRINTED IN THE UNITED STATES OF AMERICA

Contents

Preface

Since the end of World War II, Elizabethan studies have been transformed. In all areas, drama, poetry, and prose, spectacular advances in knowledge have brought new understanding and appreciation and reversed judgments that had been largely handed on from the nineteenth century. No one now would dream of castigating Elizabethan drama for its use of soliloquy and disguise, as William Archer did in 1923,[1] and modern anthologies of verse lay the emphasis quite differently from those which were in use fifty years ago.[2] As the use of conventions in drama and verse has been better understood so also has the rhetorical basis of contemporary prose. Among the books that, as a result, have come to fresh life is Sir Philip Sidney's *Arcadia*, now read with admiration and recognized as a work not only of far-reaching importance but one still charged with vitality. It remains possible for a critic to discredit Sidney's style,[3] but this view is a minority one that critical analysis and many readers reject. As for the content of *Arcadia*, the bibliography of books and articles devoted to studying this denotes by sheer size the richness that postwar readers have found in a book that T. S. Eliot described in 1933 as unreadably dull.[4]

Part of this richness derives from the amalgamation of materials that Sidney drew upon, especially for the revised version of *Arcadia*. The introductions to modern critical editions specify these sources,[5] and scholars are struck by the sophistication of his use of them and also, paradoxically, by the originality of what emerges. John O'Connor, investigating Sidney's debt to *Amadis de Gaule*, a source Sidney drew upon heavily, writes, "His plot is the result of blending, assimilating and ordering,"[6] and A. C. Hamilton, acknowledging that *Arcadia* is a "radically imitative" work, adds that it is nevertheless "radically unlike its sources."[7] The choice, disposition and remodeling of sources is a fruitful subject and an illuminating one, though Maurice Evans, like Vickers a dissentient voice in a chorus of appreciation, describes Sidney as unsuccessfully attempting to patch over "incompatible elements" from "different genres, even . . . different civilisations."[8] These and other comments, favorable or unfavorable, show at the least that, even on the lines of traditional argument relating to style and content, there is much matter in *Arcadia*.

Beyond that, however, there are further dimensions of critical study. In his *English Literature in the Sixteenth Century*, C. S. Lewis wrote, with reference to *Arcadia*, that "Sidney assumes in his readers an agreed response to certain ideals of virtue, honour, friendship and magnanimity."[9] In the last decades of the twentieth century such a statement begs nearly every possible question. Three collections of critical essays devoted to Sidney and published within the last few years illustrate clearly the tendencies of recent thinking.[10] Words are irredeemably shifty, meanings indeterminate, the records of the past unreliable because conditioned by the interests and pressures of their time. Under the influence of the various skepticisms, the inherited image of Sidney becomes a "legend" or a "myth" ripe for deconstruction, and criticism acknowledges no boundaries beyond which it is unsuitable or unhelpful to trespass. Certainly no "assumptions" about what Sidney "assumes" are acceptable, nor about absolutes of any kind, whether moral, political, or literary (such as genre, for example). The breaking of bounds is stimulating, even if at times it appears merely willful.

Given the very active state of Sidney criticism, it may be necessary to state the position from which this book is written. I find the fruits of the latest school of critical thinking only rarely persuasive, but I share at least one attitude, though with different results. I believe that, to a greater or lesser degree, critical readings of *Arcadia* are mistaken that attempt to schematize according to traditional formulas or take for granted that Sidney's point of view will necessarily coincide with accepted opinion of his day. The number of books and articles that attempt to match Sidney's thinking to a strict sixteenth-century Calvinism exemplifies one kind of approach that I believe distorts the tone and temper of Sidney's work and one that moreover, I shall argue, is unsustainable in the face of counterevidence. An instance of an approach I find limiting in another way is Nancy Lindheim's *The Structures of Sidney's Arcadia*.[11] This is a substantial book and valuable on many levels but, by laying stress on thematic and other structures, it insufficiently recognizes the exploratory modes of Sidney's thought. The revised *Arcadia*, in particular, is notable among much else for its adventurous probing and scrutiny of every aspect of human behavior as Sidney could conceive of it. The placing of the story in pre-Christian times gives him special freedom for this and he exploits it fully. The exploratory character of his work is something that should not be obscured, either by the accretions of scholarship or by critical methodologies too singlemindedly followed.

Stressing this as I do, I nevertheless believe that there is an ultimate boundary to Sidney's adventuring and that *Arcadia* draws it. The organization and orientation of the whole rests on a belief in a benevolent providence, tested rigorously but affirmed in the end and sustaining the burden of sin, error, suffering, and confusion that presses upon Arcadian lives throughout. Sidney has the confidence to include in his *Arcadia* dark, harsh, questioning, and unhappy elements, and one guarantee of this confidence is the pervasive presence of his humor. Even so subtle a critic as John Carey ignores this,[12] but it is a large contributor to the sheer enjoyability of *Arcadia*. This pleasure-giving quality derives from many features of the book, and I have tried to communicate my sense of it in what follows. By analyzing more thoroughly than previously the interlocking histories of Sidney's characters and by looking freshly at what emerges from his treatment of narrative, I hope to enhance awareness of his artistry. By discussing his depiction of the moral quality of major figures, both men and women, I hope to illuminate the spiritual background of *Arcadia* more clearly and to distinguish more carefully the degrees of shading that Sidney allows. Above all, I wish to add to appreciation of Sidney as a great and original creative talent, one of remarkable intellectual and imaginative power. Shakespeare read him and learned from him, and there should be no doubt that the writer of *Arcadia* was worthy to appear in that company.

Introduction

Sir Philip Sidney lived and died four centuries ago, a brief life of only thirty-two years, from 1554 to 1586. It was an incomplete career, like that of the Romantic poets from whom he was in most respects so vastly different. Byron died at thirty-six, Shelley at thirty, and Keats was even younger. Yet it is not common to speculate about what Sidney would have gone on to write if he had lived, as it is preeminently about Keats. Keats on his deathbed himself grieved for the work he had not the time and the maturity to do and bitterly resented his truncated life. Sidney, before ever he went to the Netherlands, shortly after to meet his death as a soldier, also felt acutely the pain of frustrated hopes and energies. His friend and mentor, the Burgundian Hubert Languet, a European diplomat of wide experience and renown, accused him of becoming slothful and he replied with some bitterness that it was only too true: "For to what purpose should our thoughts be directed to various kinds of knowledge, unless room be afforded for putting it into practice, so that public advantage may result, which in a corrupt age we cannot hope for."[1]

Sidney's frustrations, however, were unlike those of Keats in that they did not relate to books or poems he might write. If he had lived, the fulfillment he would have looked for would have been in the role of statesman guiding the destinies of his country, and attempting to cement a European Protestant alliance to curb the power of Spain and the Pope. He wrote, in part but not entirely, because his path was blocked in other directions. The bullet that broke his thigh in a minor encounter at Zutphen and led to his death three weeks later from gangrene may not have put a premature end to his work as a writer, for his achievement in that respect may very well have been in essentials complete; if we do not speculate about his unlived future as an influence and originator in the field of literature, perhaps what we must most regret is that we cannot know what the impact upon him of the unprophesiable genius of Shakespeare would have been: of the impact of Sidney upon Shakespeare something is known.

As we reflect on Sidney's life, it presents itself, like so much else, as paradoxical. On the one hand, it was a success of phenomenal proportions, drawing praise, adulation even, from innumerable sources. Great scholars and prominent statesmen, both at home and abroad—especially abroad, where he traveled extensively—responded to him with fervent admiration. Writers, scholars, explorers, men of parts in many activities, acknowledged his patronage and his example with what seems to have been genuine gratitude and praise. Through the centuries he has survived as the "preux chevalier, sans peur et sans reproche." Shelley invoked his shade to mourn the dead Adonais:

> . . . Sidney as he fought
> And as he fell and as he lived and loved
> Sublimely mild, a spirit without spot;

Yeats, lamenting that the "discourtesy of death" had overtaken Major Robert Gregory, described him as "Our Sidney and our perfect man"; Eliot, cooking eggs, reflected that:

> I shall not want honour in Heaven
> For I shall meet Sir Philip Sidney
> And have talk with Coriolanus
> And other heroes of that kidney.

If there is some irony in the Eliot reference, it is not altogether misplaced, for Sidney was not a plaster saint and his virtues are all the more striking for that.

There is abundant evidence of how greatly he impressed his contemporaries. When the news of his death reached England, the reaction can be compared with the impact of the news of the death of President John F. Kennedy in our own recent history. Like Kennedy, Sidney seemed to men of his time to offer a hope for the future, not only of his own country but of other nations too. The blow to hopes was cruel. Even Philip of Spain, who, by an irony of that century's religious turmoils was Sidney's godfather and had given him his name, was touched by it. So was Queen Elizabeth who had not treated him well, though she was also exasperated and called him "inconsiderate" for having got himself killed and so deprived her of the services of a man of rank. As legends grew around Kennedy, so they grew around Sidney, the best known, perhaps, being the story told by his friend and fellow poet, Fulke Greville, about his being carried wounded from the battlefield and calling for drink. It was brought, but as he was putting the bottle to his mouth he saw a poor soldier, fatally wounded in the same battle, being carried along and casting his eyes up at the bottle; whereupon Sidney, not drinking himself, passed the bottle over to the soldier, saying "Thy necessity is yet greater than mine."[2] This would be an appealing story told of any man at any time, but as an act of deference to a common soldier by an Elizabethan of Sidney's rank and importance it becomes truly remarkable. Lawrence Stone has drawn attention to the story of Lord Herbert of Cherbury who at one time was in danger of drowning in a storm off Dover. The ship in which he was traveling split, and a boat put out from the shore to attempt a rescue, whereupon Herbert jumped in first and with drawn sword demanded that his companion, Sir Thomas Lucy, be brought and put in the boat (Sir Thomas was very seasick at the time and incapable of making any demands on his own account). To keep his place and ensure that he was not crowded out, Herbert threatened to kill anyone else who tried to get in, and the two noblemen were rowed off in the otherwise empty boat.[3] Once safe on shore they did have the humanity to send out more boats to take off the men and horses left on the ship. Herbert himself records this episode in his autobiography. To modern minds it might appear to reflect not altogether creditably on him but evidently it did not strike him so. *Noblesse* did not so much *oblige* as take precedence, and he expected every right-thinking person to take that for granted. We mis-spend our energies if we vent our latter-day indignation upon him, but the story does throw into sharp relief the tale of Sidney and the poor soldier and the bottle of water. Sidney's contemporaries recognized in him qualities not to be found in other men, and Lord Herbert of Cherbury inadvertently provides some glimpse of what they saw. Certainly, imaginative understanding of other people's situations and a wide sympathy are qualities notably present in Sidney's writings, and these constitute the most intimate evidence there is of him as he was and as he lived.

He had no Boswell and the only recorded example of his conversation is, curiously enough, on the subject of why there are no wolves in England, a question put to him round a dinner table in Prague (or it might have been Nürnberg). It is not without its interest, but the real flavor of his conversation as it must have been among a close circle is best preserved in his critical essay, *An Apology for Poetry*. There to relish is the cultivated mind, the well-formed intelligence, the serious-minded man who thoroughly believed that the final end of learning is "to lead and draw us to as high a perfection as our degenerate souls, made worse by their clayey lodgings, can be capable of."[4] But there is also the lightness of touch; the courtesy in argument; the self-deprecating humor; the irony, amusing but not cruel, that is shrewdly directed at opponents; and there is the warmth of imagination that lights up the language and gives vigor to the ideas.

To read the *Apology* is to gain some insight into how Sidney charmed by his personality as well as impressed by his intellectual and other gifts.

All this is to confirm his life as a success story, but from another point of view it was a dismal failure. In 1581 he appeared at a court tournament with the word "speravi" inscribed on his shield but crossed out. The immediate reason for this canceled hope was the birth of a son to his uncle, Robert Dudley, Earl of Leicester, a child who at once supplanted Sidney as heir to both his uncles, Leicester and Warwick—in point of fact the child died within a few years. But the shield and its legend had a wider significance than that, for disappointed hope became a keynote of his life after a brilliant beginning when a career of superlative distinction seemed to be open to him. Elizabeth thought him, or purported to think him, too ambitious. The impression he made on others threatened in her eyes to make him too powerful. Glittering foreign marriages were proposed for him, among them William of Orange offered a match with his eldest daughter, together with the Lordship of Holland and Zealand. Elizabeth disapproved of such connections, but Sidney's eligibility increased her sense that he needed to be kept on a strong leash. A young man with such friends, nobly connected at home, highly intelligent, burning with zeal to promote a dynamic policy toward the threat posed by Spain to the Protestant cause in Europe, and well prepared for a role on the European stage—such a man seriously threatened the balancing act that by policy and instinct she maintained through forty-five arduous years. She appointed him to no post commensurate with his gifts, and she allowed him to rusticate at the great house at Wilton that belonged to his much-loved sister, the Countess of Pembroke. In his frustration he tried to abscond, to sail with Drake to the new world, there perhaps to found a colony and find that scope for his energy and ideas which was denied him in England; but Elizabeth heard about it and hauled him back and sent him instead to the Netherlands as Governor of Flushing.

Flushing was a key position in the Netherlands struggle against Spain, and the moment was a critical one. William of Orange had been assassinated in 1584 and the English feared that Spain would seize the opportunity to use the Netherlands as a springboard for invasion. It was essential to strengthen English aid to the Dutch, but when Sidney arrived in Flushing it was undermanned, the troops unpaid, and the defenses dilapidated. From November 1585, when he arrived, till September 1586, when he received his wound, Sidney struggled grimly to improve the situation in the face of stubborn noncooperation from the government at home. In March 1586 he wrote to Sir Francis Walsingham, Elizabeth's Secretary of State whose daughter, Frances, Sidney had married in 1583. This is a letter that James Osborn, in his 1972 biography, calls, with reason, perhaps the finest he ever wrote.[5] It is indeed a splendid and moving letter, full of courage and Christian confidence but full also of weariness and disillusion. "I think a wyse and constant man ought never to greeve whyle he doth play as a man may sai his own part truly though others be out," he writes. The Queen, he knows, is willing to interpret all he does in a wrong sense and, he adds, "I understand I am called very ambitious and prowd at home, but certainly if thei knew my ha[rt] thei woold not altogether so judg me."[6] This is a sad letter written by a man who strongly suspects that disgrace and reproach are to be his reward for all he does but who has settled with himself, nevertheless, to do his duty with constancy and courage, come what may. When he died, he must have felt, like Keats after him, that his name was writ in water.

It was not so of course. Though the spectacular career never developed, legends of a glorious life accrued to his personality, and his writing survived. This was not where he would have chosen to devote his main energies; it was not where he intended to make his real mark; but it was there that he has made his greatest contribution to the honor of his country, which he so much wished to serve, and there that his achievement not only endures but is now estimated more highly than at any time since his own day. A fuller understanding and appreciation of Sidney as a writer is now in process of developing, one of the most welcome fruits of the scholarly and critical work devoted to the sixteenth century since the last war.

As a very young man, in the intervals of attendance at Court and travels overseas, Sidney, with his friends Fulke Greville and Edward Dyer, tried their hands at poetry. It was a courtly accomplishment, part of the modern refinement taught by Castiglione and practiced with success in Italy and France, but English poets had failed to master the language and the rhythms of the modern vernacular and Sidney felt it a disgrace that his countrymen should be outpaced by others. The situation was very soon to change. In the 1590s the tongues of English poets were unloosed and the brief but potent golden age dawned. John Buxton has no hesitation in saying that the flowering of English poetry in the last ten years of the sixteenth century was not, as he writes, "some haphazard accident, due to the fortuitous collocation of poetic genius in that decade," but it was brought about principally by the skill and insight of Sidney and his companions, Greville and Dyer.[7] What the contribution of Dyer was, it is impossible fully to estimate now, for its nature and extent are uncertain. As for Greville, he was a man of powerful intellect who struck out his own poetic style, especially after Sidney's death. He was a man who, as he said, knew the world and believed in God, a combination of cynicism and faith that produced striking effects. Greville's poetry, impressive as much of it is, is inevitably too strongly individualistic to have been a far-reaching influence. But the combination of these three minds working on the possibilities of modern poetry fired Sidney in particular to compose works of historically great importance and, beyond that, works that delight the imagination and engage the attention down to our own day.

With hindsight, Sidney's writing career can be plotted as an orderly sequence. He begins with prentice pieces: an entertainment for the Queen, *The Lady of May*, experiments in classical scansion, forming part of his joint endeavor with Greville and Dyer to find the secret of English versification, and a number of miscellaneous poems. In the early 1580s he clears his mind about what he is doing and the object of it by composing his *Apology for Poetry* in which he claims that poetry is worth the best efforts of good men and good minds. Then he goes on to write a sonnet sequence, *Astrophil and Stella*, the first such sequence in English, challenging comparison with Petrarch and the Petrarchists of Italy and France. Finally, to demonstrate the versatility of English in both prose and verse, he composes a work of epic scope and ambition, *Arcadia*, a prose romance interspersed with verse eclogues. This account has some truth but is misleading. In the first place, there is no question of Sidney having planned a writing career. In his "idle" times he had "slipped into the title of a poet," as he puts it in the *Apology*, but his ambitions were directed elsewhere. Literature was a private occupation for his unemployed hours, though this is not to say that he did not take it seriously both as part of a nation's claim to greatness and as a liberation of the individual spirit. Secondly, his writings do not follow in a straight sequential line but overlap—we need to remember that a great deal of creative energy is packed into a handful of years. This fact itself leads to the third and most important point, that the works grow out of each other, not according to a predetermined scheme but in response to the opening of fresh horizons as Sidney feels the stir of new creative powers awakened to meet the challenge of newly recognized possibilities.

He was denied the chance to create a new world across the sea, but he could create a world on paper: it remains to ask what kind of world that was, and the rest of this book will be devoted to delineating its outstanding features. The focus of attention will be on *Arcadia*, in the writing of which Sidney's gifts reached their fullest maturity. It is an immensely entertaining and immensely complex work, but it is not always well read and has perhaps not yet been fully appreciated. *Astrophil and Stella* has long been given its due importance as the first Elizabethan sonnet sequence, and critical attention in recent years has exposed it to feminist, materialist, and other fashionable modes of analysis; but in one important respect it is a staging post on the way to *New Arcadia*, and it is as such that it will be discussed here.

Some preliminaries about the history of *Arcadia* need to be dealt with before the critical account can begin. Sidney began writing *Arcadia* between 1577 and 1580 and dedicated it to his sister, the young and, in 1577, newly married Countess of Pembroke. The dedication takes the form of an affectionate, intimate letter to this "most dear, and most worthy to be most dear lady" and in it Sidney, himself in his early twenties, apologizes for it as a "trifle, and that triflingly handled." He asks her indulgence for its deficiencies, considering how and why it was composed:

> Your dear self can best witness the manner, being done in loose sheets of paper, most of it in your presence; the rest by sheets sent unto you as fast as they were done. Read it, then, at your idle times, and the follies your good judgement will find in it blame not, but laugh at.

The text thus dedicated to the Countess is usually known as *Old Arcadia*, and this is only the beginning of *Arcadia*'s history. Prepared as he was by birth and training to expect a responsible and prominent role in the affairs of his country, Sidney found himself balked at every turn. In what has traditionally been known as *A Life of Sidney* (the most recent editor prefers the title *A Dedication to Sir Philip Sidney*) his friend, Fulke Greville, recorded how he himself sought to break out of the constrictions of life at Elizabeth's court by taking service overseas, until the Queen's displeasure forced him to accept that the best course was to make the most he could of whatever channels she would leave open to him. In some such spirit Sidney took up his *Old Arcadia* and began to rewrite it, turning it from the "idle work" of its first composition into a repository for all the experience he had acquired and filling it with intellectual and moral energy. He enlarged and complicated the original text very much, introducing a large company of additional characters and engaging them in a multiplicity of intricately interwoven episodes. Though his readers would still find plenty to entertain and amuse them, they would also see that his book could no longer be described, even with graceful modesty, as a "trifle . . . triflingly handled."

This revision of *Arcadia*, however, is unfinished. Sidney had rewritten books 1 and 2 of the original and had composed a considerable part of an entirely new book 3 when he was appointed Governor of Flushing. Before he left, he gave a manuscript of the uncompleted revision of *Arcadia* to Greville, for safekeeping until his return; but he never returned. In October 1586 he was wounded in a minor action and died three weeks later, after much suffering.

Sidney himself did not consider publishing his work, nor was he likely to have done so if he had lived. Publication was for professional writers competing in the marketplace, and the works of gentleman amateurs gained their readers by circulation of manuscripts among their peers and dependants. All the same, manuscripts tended to get into the hands of printers who saw no reason why they should not print and make money from them. One such acquired a manuscript of *Old Arcadia*, to the alarm of Fulke Greville, and he wrote to Sidney's father-in-law, Sir Francis Walsingham, a month after Sidney's death, to warn him that a pirated edition was in the offing.[8] This unauthorized publication was stopped, but to protect the text from the botching it might receive at some future time in less careful hands than his own, Greville in 1590 published the manuscript that Sidney had entrusted to him when he left for Holland. He was scrupulous in his dealing with it, allowing the text to break off in the middle of a sentence somewhere in the new book 3 just as Sidney had left it, but he accepted the need for a degree of editorial initiative. Either he, or more likely, his assistant Dr. Matthew Gwinne (or perhaps John Florio) made chapter divisions and headed each one with a little synopsis of the matter contained within it. This, as an introductory note to the edition explains, is "for the more ease of the Readers," an interesting acknowledgment of the complexity of Sidney's narrative methods in the revision, such that even readers accustomed to the forms on which Sidney was drawing would require some help: this was no ordinary work of so familiar a kind that it could be taken in at once. Decisions had also to be made about the choice and disposition of the poems in the pastoral interludes (eclogues) for Sidney, we are told, had himself deferred decision on these matters until he had finished the whole work. The edition of 1590 was followed by a second one in 1593, under the care of the Countess of Pembroke herself, assisted by Hugh Sanford, a tutor and secretary in her household. The 1593 edition republishes the revised text to the point where it breaks off but then adds to it the later phases of the story from a manuscript of the *Old Arcadia*. The chapter readings of 1590 are omitted from this edition, and different decisions are taken about the choice and placing of the poems. Putting together the revised and unrevised texts produces an inevitable bump at the point where the broken-off new book 3 meets the text of *Old Arcadia*, but in spite of this, other editions of the composite *Arcadia* followed. Then, after an interval, Sir William Alexander, Scottish poet and writer of closet (i.e., nontheatrical) drama, a genre favored by the Countess, undertook to write a bridging passage, linking the two portions of text together. He did so with skill and success enough to bring it about that this by now tripartite text, first published in 1621, held the imagination of readers for more than a century.

The textual complications of *Arcadia* do not stop there. For nearly three hundred years it was believed that all that survived of *Old Arcadia* was that part of it which the Countess of Pembroke had incorporated into the 1593 edition, but in the early years of this century, three manuscripts came to light, and subsequently another six. It then became apparent that there were some considerable discrepancies between the text represented by these manuscripts and the text of the later books as published in 1593. Some of them could be explained as editorial adjustments of a legitimate kind to take account of the revisions of books 1, 2, and 3, but early commentators were inclined to suspect that Lady Pembroke had gone much further than that and made her own revisions of her brother's work. In the *Old Arcadia* manuscripts both Pyrocles and Musidorus, the young and princely heroes, either intend, or actually achieve, sexual consummation before marriage with the princesses Pamela and Philoclea, but in the printed text the relevant scenes are toned down and become innocent. Did Lady Pembroke make the changes on her own initiative so as not to offend against propriety? Ringler in his edition of Sidney's *Poems* argued strongly that she did not. It is known from Greville's letter to Walsingham that Sidney had left with his manuscripts some directions for alterations to be made, and it is virtually certain that the directions relate to these passages and another extensive piece of rewriting in book 5, relating to Euarchus's journey to Arcadia. That these revisions in the later books of the 1593 edition were in accordance with Sidney's wishes and instructions is now generally accepted, and indeed, a careful reading of *New Arcadia* makes it an inescapable conclusion.

In the light of all the complexities of its composition and transmission, however, to speak of reading *Arcadia* is to beg a question: what is *Arcadia?* William Alexander's bridge passage can be disregarded, but even so we are left with one complete text that the author wished to replace by another; part of a second that presumably he was satisfied with; and part of a third, the old books 3, 4, and 5, in a process of transition from stage one to stage two. Ringler speaks of "continuous copy" (p. 369), and the latest editor identifies five states of the text. Modern Shakespeareans are much interested in the idea of fluid texts, plays constantly in a process of transformation under the influence of performance and not to be thought of, consequently, as being once and for all final and definite. The situation has disadvantages for critical study but also advantages. In relation to *Arcadia* it is certainly to be counted as a privilege that we can see a writer and his work growing before our eyes, a writer, moreover, who is at all stages a highly accomplished artist. The *Old Arcadia*, out of which *New Arcadia* grew, was itself a remarkable production, "a composition more carefully structured and more artfully executed than anything in English of its time," writes Ringler (p. 383), and Jean Robertson, pointing out the Terentian structure of *Old Arcadia* in five books, or acts, and its kinship with tragicomedy, comments that "Sidney had planned his five-act drama with extreme care; and he triumphantly carried out his intentions with unflagging execution right through to the final scene."[9] The editor of the World's Classics edition, Katherine Duncan-Jones, appears to give pride of place to the earlier text rather than the later.

Nevertheless, Sidney wanted to go beyond the early text. He did not discard *Old Arcadia,* for he retained most of the early writing in his revision, but he opened it out, finding in the original narrative possibilities of development that make it much more substantial and exploring its implications more fully and more minutely. Some elements in the progress of his thinking can be deduced with confidence. The directions he left for amendments in the later books show that he wished to remove from the princes the odium of sexual seduction. This was not necessarily because of enhanced prudishness. In *Amadis de Gaule*, a source he drew on heavily for a number of episodes in his story, heroines accept extramarital embraces with considerable unconcern and Sidney did not think that the moral value of the work was diminished thereby.[10] The reasons for the changes must have been intellectual and artistic ones, a recognition that the newly extensive and very thoughtful analysis of kinds of love, and behavior in love, made the original treatment of the scene in Philoclea's bedroom and Musidorus's behavior during his elopement with Pamela inappropriate. By this time Sidney has deepened his presentation of Pyrocles and Musidorus by setting them into significant relation with other characters who do not appear in *Old Arcadia*, and for this reason also the earlier versions of the scenes become not merely unsuitable but actually at odds with later developments.

At what point Sidney began to see the possibilities of his story opening out—after he had completed the first version or even while he was writing it—is a question of some importance for the reading of *New Arcadia*. *Old Arcadia* ends in a trial in which the youthful loves of the princes and princesses, the middle-aged passion of Gynecia, and the aged follies of Basilius are subjected to intense critical scrutiny. Basilius appears to be dead; Pyrocles and Musidorus and Gynecia are threatened with total disgrace and execution; Philanax, the wise and cool-headed counselor, becomes a man rabidly set on revenge; Euarchus, the man famous for his justice and probity, is subjected to searching and finally agonizing tests. All the principal characters come under extreme pressure in which they are forced to acknowledge truths about themselves, whether for good or ill. The political dimension of Arcadian affairs also comes to the fore more prominently than before, as the personal entanglements of the Arcadian royal family produce disorder in the state and open the way both for internal dissension and for the threat of foreign invasion. The perspectives into character that the trial brings into view, the opening of urgent questions of government, the consideration of the relations of justice and mercy, the strengths and the limitations of law, all this becomes the material of major expansions in the revised books 1, 2, and 3. Everything suggests that *Old Arcadia*, in effect, is turning into *New Arcadia* in its last books and that the revision of the earlier parts is undertaken in the light of *Old Arcadia* books 4 and 5. Hugh Sanford, introducing the 1593 edition, which was produced under the Countess of Pembroke's supervision, wrote that the reader would find there a conclusion, not the perfection of *Arcadia*, adding that it was constructed out of "the Author's own writings, or knowen determinations," these known "determinations" being presumably the directions for amendment referred to by Greville. "The conclusion not the perfection" is a vague enough phrase to be capable of more than one interpretation, but Sanford's remarks do not eliminate the possibility that the 1593 text of the trial and surrounding circumstances represents essentially what Sidney meant to stand, though it lacks the "perfecting" he would have given to it. Arguments that this is so will be developed in the course of this book.

What Sidney accomplished in his revision of *Arcadia* and how it should be estimated, what the moral quality of the princes is, and how the reader should understand the final judgment of the trial scene are questions to be dealt with in the following chapters. It is impossible to give in summary form an account of all the interlocking narratives that make up *New Arcadia*, but these are all attached in one way or another to the main narrative line as it is pursued without the later accretions in *Old Arcadia*. The following is a brief account:

Basilius, ruler of Arcadia, has received an oracular prediction that distressing events are about to happen in the lives of himself and his family. In the hope of averting them, he retires with his wife,

Gynecia, and his two daughters, Pamela, the elder and his heir, and Philoclea, to a forest. Government of the country is left in the hands of a wise counselor, Philanax. Since the predicted events seem to revolve largely around prospective suitors of his daughters and also because usurpation by a stranger seems threatened, he forbids access to the lodges where he settles except by a trusted herdsman, called Dametas, his wife, Miso, and their daughter, Mopsa. Certain selected shepherds are also allowed to be in the vicinity of the lodges. Pamela is put in the care of Dametas and his family in one lodge, while Basilius, his wife, and younger daughter live in the other. Pyrocles and Musidorus, two young princes, after many adventures round the shores of the eastern Mediterranean, arrive in Arcadia. There Pyrocles, the younger, sees a portrait of Philoclea and falls in love with her. He determines to dress up as an Amazon warrior and, as a woman, ingratiate himself with Basilius and his family in order to get permission to be near Philoclea in the hope of being able to woo her. Musidorus, slightly older than Pyrocles, disapproves of this course of action and has no sympathy with the idea of romantic love. He changes his mind, however, when he sees Pamela by chance and falls deeply in love with her. To be admitted to the royal circle he too disguises himself, as a shepherd, and takes service with Dametas. Basilius, an old man and a foolish one, himself succumbs to the charms of the supposed Amazon and begins to court the supposed "her." Gynecia, his wife, who is very much younger than her husband and a great deal more intelligent, soon sees through Pyrocles' disguise and conceives an ungovernable passion for him as a young man. Meanwhile Philoclea is too young and innocent to suspect anything but becomes confused and disturbed by the unfamiliar emotions she begins to feel in the presence of the Amazon. Eventually, Musidorus, having managed to convey to Pamela his real identity and won her heart, decides that there is nothing to do but elope with her and, on arriving in his own country, to marry her and hope that Basilius will then accept the situation and agree also to the marriage of Pyrocles and Philoclea; if not, Musidorus is prepared to use force to ensure the success of Pyrocles' affairs. Pyrocles by this point has also been driven to desperation because, although Philoclea now knows who he is and loves him, there seems no prospect of bringing his suit to fruition, and in the meantime both Basilius and Gynecia are pressing him hard for the satisfaction of their own unruly desires. By a subterfuge he contrives that they will both spend a night together in a cave, each supposing that the assignation is in fact with him. Seizing this opportunity, he himself goes to Philoclea, anticipating their marriage, according to the manuscripts of *Old Arcadia;* not so in the printed text of 1593 where he merely tries to persuade her to run away with him. He is not now in his Amazon dress, and in the morning he is seen by Dametas who at once broadcasts the information that the supposed lady warrior is in fact a man. Musidorus's plans are also ruined when he and Pamela are captured by a group of former rebels who bring them back to the lodges in the hope of buying their way back into Basilius's favor by so doing. Basilius, however, waking in the morning after his night in the cave and finding that it was, in fact, his wife whom he had been enthusiastically embracing and not, as he thought, a young mistress, has drunk a potion given him by Gynecia. She has not intended malice but, after drinking, Basilius falls as though dead and she believes that she must inadvertently have given him poison. Gynecia and the two princes are all arrested by Philanax and brought to trial, Gynecia on a charge of murdering the king, and the princes on charges of complicity in the murder and of seeking to abduct the heir to the throne and seducing her sister. They are tried by Euarchus, King of Macedonia, who by chance has arrived in Arcadia and who has a reputation as a most incorruptible and upright judge. He finds all three guilty as charged and sentences them to various forms of execution. It is then discovered, what has hitherto not been known to any of them, that Pyrocles is Euachus's own son whom he has not seen for many years and that Musidorus is his nephew. Although it wrings his heart to decide so, he insists that the sentences must stand in spite of his close kinship with the princes. At this point, the apparently dead body of Basilius begins to stir, and it transpires that the potion was not deadly after all but a draught rather like that which Friar Lawrence gives to Juliet in *Romeo and Juliet*. Basilius, reviving, countermands the sentences, Gynecia is restored to honor, and the princes and princesses are married.

This in barest outline is the story of *Arcadia* as it is told in both versions, but there is one major addition to *New Arcadia* that needs to be noted because it is of great importance. This is the material of the new book 3, the book that remained incomplete when Sidney left for Holland. In *New Arcadia*, book 3, Cecropia, Basilius's sister-in-law (a new character) has the princesses, Pamela and Philoclea, kidnapped. She is ambitious for her son, Amphialus (another new character) to inherit the throne of Arcadia, and she hopes that, either by the death of both princesses or by the marriage of one of them to Amphialus, his succession may be assured. Pyrocles, as Zelmane the Amazon, is captured along with the princesses but is unable to assist them since they are locked in separate rooms and he has no weapon. Amphialus, though he deplores the violence done, is desperately in love with Philoclea and cannot find it in his heart to let her leave his castle.

While she is there he hopes to be able to make progress in his suit to her. He is, however, very much occupied with other matters, first with arranging for the defense of his castle against the attack he expects Basilius to make on it, and then with fighting a succession of battles and single combats with the forces that Basilius pits against him in his efforts to release the prisoners. In a climactic fight with Musidorus, Amphialus is badly wunded, and Cecropia, fearing that a combination of his wounds and his frustrated love will kill him, takes brutal measures to attempt to break the princesses' spirit. She goes so far as torture and the staging of mock executions in an attempt to break down the resistance of one of them—she is indifferent which— so that she can offer comfort to Amphialus. Whichever sister suc- cumbs, Cecropia intends to have the other murdered. The sisters continue to resist all pressures, Amphialus at last discovers how they have been treated and in shame and anger reviles his mother. She, retreating before him, steps back and falls from the roof where they are both standing. She dies and Amphialus, when the revision breaks off, is at death's door, but there is some hope that he may eventually recover.

All this is fresh matter in *New Arcadia*, and there is a considerable gap between the final episodes of Book 3 and the later events as they are picked up from *Old Arcadia*.

Editions used in this study are: *The Countess of Pembroke's Arcadia (The Old Arcadia)*, ed. Jean Robertson (Oxford, 1973); *Arcadia*, ed. Maurice Evans (Penguin, 1977); and *The Countess of Pembroke's Arcadia (The New Arcadia)*, ed. Victor Skretkowicz (Oxford, 1987). References are given as NA (for *New Arcadia*), OA (for *Old Arcadia*), and P (for the Penguin edition).

The eclogues, variously published in the 1590 and 1593 editions, are not considered in this study since Sidney's intentions for their placing are not clear and there is no assurance that what we have would have been retained or that others might not have been added. In these circumstances, speculation about their function and signifi- cance must be excessively hypothetical.

Sir Philip Sidney
and *Arcadia*

1
Heroes and Heroics

The roots of characterization in *Arcadia* lie in the type figures of medieval narrative, characters traditionally conceived as examples of good and bad qualities; but the growth from these roots is very impressive. Sidney adds individualizing touches that give a degree of personal life, and beyond this, moral shadings and discriminations are so fine and sensitively observed as to be genuine contributions to psychological understanding. He creates figures who, in spite of their romantic and chivalric background, are susceptible of discussion as authentic natures, and he weaves together with extraordinary skill personal histories and wider patterns of meaning so that each feeds and illuminates the other. The most remarkable example of this process is the figure of Amphialus, a fresh and vitally important creation in the revised *Arcadia*. Amphialus is not only a subtle character study in himself but also, by what he is and what he does, he is the key to the moral outlook of the revised text and, in particular, to the view that Sidney intended his readers to take of the heroes, Pyrocles and Musidorus.

Sidney has many portraits of lovers in *New Arcadia*, and they range through most degrees of crudity and refinement, but Amphialus is of special importance because he is an heroic figure who might well compete with Pyrocles and Musidorus for the reader's sympathy and admiration. In fact, his principal function in *New Arcadia*'s overall organization is to clear the princes of any ambiguity that may have attached to their behavior in *Old Arcadia*. Amphialus is a man of the same stamp as Pyrocles and Musidorus, but as a lover, he takes wrong ways. As a direct result of this he defies his duty as a subject and leads a rebellion against his king. He is responsible for the loss of many lives and in particular for the deaths of Argalus and Parthenia, Argalus a nobler man than he and one who, together with his wife, is capable also of a nobler love. By demonstrating his affinities with Pyrocles and Musidorus and yet discriminating him from them, Sidney clarifies and enhances the status of his central figures. Analysis of the nature and functions of the characterization of the hero figures of the revised

Arcadia should begin, therefore, with consideration of Amphialus and the part he plays.

There are many aspects of Amphialus that are very attractive. His deep distress at his unwilling responsibility for the deaths of Philoxenus and his father, his sad and heart-felt devotion to Philoclea and Sidney's insistence on his courage, courtesy, and nobility all predispose the reader to offer him sympathy and to wish him well. He may readily appear to be a tragic figure, victim of a hostile fate that consistently thwarts his good intentions and perverts his actions so that, against his will, they produce destruction; but this is not an adequate response to all Sidney presents. The scene with Cecropia, his mother, when she tells him of her attempts to murder Basilius and his wife and of the kidnapping of the princesses, makes it clear that there are other factors operating to determine Amphialus's misfortunes than simply a malign destiny. The conversation between mother and son proceeds in part like this:

> "Alas," said Amphialus, "my heart would fain yield you thanks for setting me in the way of felicity, but that fear kills them in me before they are fully born; for if Philoclea be displeased, how can I be pleased; if she count it unkindness, shall I give tokens of kindness? Perchance she condemns me of this action and shall I triumph? Perchance she drowns now the beauties I love with sorrowful tears and where is then my rejoicing?"
>
> "You have reason," said Cecropia, with a feigned gravity. "I will therefore send her away presently, that her contentment may be recovered."
>
> "No, good mother," said Amphialus, "since she is here I would not for my life constrain presence but rather would I die than consent to absence."
>
> "Pretty intricate follies," said Cecropia. (NA, 320; P, 447)

This is a brilliant and important piece of dialogue. Cecropia's mordantly ironic style is characteristic of her sharp unsentimental mind, and it throws up clearly the less than satisfactory nature of Amphialus's response to the kidnapping of the princesses. He deplores it, but only because it may damage his chances with Philoclea. In the hope that it may, in fact, help him, he drops his resistance and reconciles himself to the violation of Philoclea's dignity and the denial of her freedom. He wraps an unjustifiable situation in words of courtly gallantry: "I will think myself highly entitled, if I may be once by Philoclea accepted for a servant," on which Cecropia's acid "Pretty intricate follies" is fair comment.

If the point is missed here, it is made quite explicit by Philoclea herself when Amphialus speaks in the same language to her: "You entitle yourself my slave, but I am sure I am yours," she tells him and adds: "If then violence, injury, terror, and depriving of that which is more dear than life itself, liberty, be fit orators for affection, you may expect that I will be easily persuaded" (NA, 322; P, 449–50). This is a damaging commentary on his protestations of love and gallantry, but Amphialus seeks again to dress the reality in a form of words that minimizes his own responsibility: "It is love, it is love, not I which disobey you." The language gets out of hand, however, and conveys more than Amphialus means it to: "There is no other remedy but that you some way vouchsafe to satisfy this love's vehemency which, since it grew in yourself, without question you shall find it (far more than I) tractable." Philoclea, not unnaturally, understands this as a threat of violence, and Amphialus is obliged to swear categorically that he will never attempt to force her. It is a disturbing position for the noble Amphialus to find himself in but not undeserved. His lack of reaction to his mother's disgraceful revelations and his failure to repudiate her offense toward the princesses has already indicated that, on him as on her, *realpolitik*, the politics of power, have a considerable hold. He has finer feelings than Cecropia and moral scruples that she entirely lacks, but when his strongest feelings are in question he is willing to take advantage of the opportunities afforded by power and, so far as he can, to disguise from himself what he is doing.

Sidney makes the same point in another way when, following the conversation with his mother, Amphialus prepares for his interview with Philoclea. He takes the utmost care over his costume, anxiously considering, among other points, a judicious choice of color. He fears that "if gay, he might seem to glory in his injury [i.e. the injury he has done her] and her wrong; if mourning, it might strike some evil presage into her of her fortune." Eventually he arrives at a satisfactory combination of garments and jewels, but in making his way to the room where Philoclea is imprisoned, he cannot help limping slightly, the result of the wound he has sustained from Zelmane/Pyrocles: "but he strave to give the best grace he could unto his halting" (NA, 321; P, 448). In this passage, where every appearance is understood as signifying a moral condition, Amphialus's "halting," which all his grace cannot conceal, is emblematic of a moral disablement undermining all he does. The reader is aware also, as Amphialus himself is not, that the "Amazon" has inflicted another wound on him that will be a permanent impediment to his attempts to ingratiate himself with Philoclea for it is Pyrocles who will win her heart.[1]

The same kind of picture of the contamination of great ability and noble virtues by a position of moral weakness is presented by Amphialus's handling of the military and political consequences of the abduction of the princesses. It also demonstrates that Amphialus is a master of *realpolitik* in the literal sense. "When Shakespeare first responded to the impact of the machiavellian in politics, he produced Richard III, something raw and callow compared with the conception of Amphialus," John Danby writes.[2] The vitality of Richard and his mockingly theatrical schemes for carving his way to power certainly seem unsophisticated when matched against the policy of Amphialus. Richard understands the value of propaganda, especially in bolstering a weak case, and instructs Buckingham to fill the ears of the Lord Mayor and the citizens with tales of Edward IV's promiscuity and to insinuate the doubtful legitimacy of his children. He is to go so far as to throw doubt on Edward's own legitimacy—though even Richard quails slightly at the thought of the Duchess of York's likely reaction and he dare not encourage Buckingham to urge this story very strongly (act 2, scene 5). Amphialus, far from being inhibited by his mother, is encouraged and instructed by her and proves to be an accomplished pupil. His propaganda justifying his defiance of Basilius is clever and plausible, claiming that the incarceration of the princesses is undertaken for their good and the good of the state, calling on all patriots and lovers of justice to defend him in his course of action and declaring his intention to defend himself, by force of arms if need be. By an adroit sleight of hand he identifies the real public enemy as Philanax, Basilius's chief counselor, and pretends that he himself is making war, not on the king, but on this man, whom he presents as a false counselor. Meanwhile he takes carefully thought-out measures to enhance the security of his castle, paying particular attention to the fitting of the right men to the right tasks for he well understands that "in the art of man stood the quintessence and ruling skill of all prosperous government, either peaceable or military" (NA, 327; P, 454).

Sidney's account of Amphialus's conduct at this point in his affairs is full of interest. Whether rebellion against a lawful monarch was ever justified and, if so, in what circumstances, was a question of much more than theoretic interest in the sixteenth century, and Amphialus's justification of his course of action lies close to lines of argument followed by Huguenot thinkers with which Sidney was well acquainted.[3] The closely detailed account of Amphialus's presentation of his case and the equally precise description of his disposition of men and resources are similarly related to contemporary affairs and in particular to Sidney's own interests. He had studied long and thoroughly to fit himself for the role of statesman, which, in his day, required both political and military expertise, and in *Arcadia* he works out possible courses of action in many varieties of situation. He is especially interested in the variant forms in which challenge to constituted authority may come. He studies the roots of it in rebellion against tyranny, as, for example, when the Helots rebel against the Lacedemonians and are supported by Pyrocles and Musidorus; or in a popular uprising stirred by agitators and quelled by Zelmane's use of skilful oratory; or, as in the present instance, in a personal challenge by a strong rival who fortifies his claim to be acting in defense of the public interest by his own royal blood and close kinship to the crown. He examines the ways in which rebellion is prosecuted or contained and the various skills involved, and there is no doubt that he presents Amphialus as very skilful indeed. Much of what he does constitutes the actions of an ideal commander: "himself rather instructing by example than precept, being neither more sparing in travail nor spending in diet than the meanest soldier; his hand and body disdaining no base matters nor shrinking from the heavy" (NA, 328; P, 455). Yet the sense that all this is based on a rotten foundation is never for long out of account, and Amphialus himself foresees that there can only be a collapse. He congratulates himself on all he does and all he is willing to dare in the name of love, but at once the premonition strikes him that his passion for Philoclea will be his "destruction." He turns in his misery to "the comfort and counsel" of his mother (NA, 329; P, 457), and as the reader of *New Arcadia* recognizes, there can be no more tainted source than that.

The sophistication of Amphialus's propaganda and the skill and judiciousness of the measures he takes for his defense are admirable, but the brutal reality of the situation is not allowed long to remain out of sight and the consequences of the kidnapping become increasingly horrifying. In the first attack launched by Basilius on Amphialus's stronghold, Amphialus kills Agenor, a young man full of hope and zest, "lately grown a lover," and of all Basilius's army "the most beautiful" (NA, 339; P, 467). Amphialus, noticing his youth and good looks, intends to spare him, but his lance shivers and the splinters devastate his face. In revenge Philanax kills Ismenus, Amphialus's devoted page. Like Antenor, he is young and handsome and, like Amphialus, Philanax's first impulse is to spare him. But violence begets violence, and seeing the dead body of Agenor, his own young brother, Philanax puts away mercy, saying to himself "Let other mothers bewail an untimely death as well as mine."

The battle is full of horror and monstrosity. Limbs are detached from their bodies and dead horses lie on top of those who should be their riders. The earth is deprived of its function of providing burial for men and is itself buried under the numbers of the slain. All this

reversal of the natural order of things is epitomized by the story of
Polycrates, a coward whose head Amphialus strikes off:

> where, with the convulsions of death setting his spurs to his horse, he gave
> so brave a charge upon the enemy as it grew a proverb that Polycrates was
> only valiant after his head was off. (NA, 324; P, 470)

There are other descriptions of conflict in *New Arcadia*, but none
that strikes the same notes as these. Perversion, delusion, unintended
but nonetheless cruel slaughter of the young, the beautiful and the
loving; these are the keynotes of it, and its significance in relation to
Amphialus's position is not to be overlooked. He has set himself upon
a destructive path in breach of natural and legal authority, and he
persists in it: abuse of natural law and perversion follow.

In spite of the horrors into which he is being led, Amphialus will
not withdraw. Basilius is ready to forgive, taking a lenient view of a
young man's weaknesses, but Amphialus rejects the offer of reinstate-
ment with "disdainful choler." Another attempt to deflect him from
his destructive course is made a little later by the noble knight
Argalus.

Argalus is lately married to his beloved Parthenia, and Sidney
paints a touching picture of their domestic happiness at the moment
when it is about to be destroyed forever by the entrance of a mes-
senger from Basilius calling upon Argalus to take up arms against
Amphialus (NA, 371–72; P, 501) Into this idyll the bloodshed and
brutality of Amphialus's war intrude. Before he fights, Argalus attempts to persuade Amphialus to end his rebellion, release the princesses, and submit to the authority of Basilius, but Amphialus is as
little responsive now as he was before. The single combat that follows
expands and underlines the horrors of the first battle between the
armies.

Argalus is the truly noble knight, the equal of Pyrocles and Musidorus and Amphialus in valiant deeds but more mature than they in
manner and experience. He and his wife, Parthenia, exemplify an
ideal marriage preceded by a courtship in which both have displayed
heroic constancy and courage. Parthenia loses her beauty by the
malice of a rejected suitor, but Argalus, recovering quickly from his
first shock at the transformation, woos her with even more ardor and
tenderness than before. To save him, as she thinks, from an unworthy
match, she disappears, leaving him free to make another choice.
Sometime later a young woman comes to him, looking very much
like, only more beautiful than, the original Parthenia. Parthenia has
died, she tells him, but it was her dying wish that Argalus should wed

the second woman, her double. Argalus refuses and looks forward to his own death:

> I hope I shall not long tarry after her, with whose beauty if I had only been in love, I should be so with you who have the same beauty. But it was Parthenia's self I loved and love, which no likeness can make one, no commandment dissolve, no foulness defile, nor no death finish. (NA, 44; P, 105)

The lady then reveals herself to be in fact Parthenia, miraculously cured of her disfigurement at the court of Queen Helen of Corinth, and Argalus and Parthenia are joyfully united.

The utter unselfishness of these lovers, their total subordination of all selfish interest to the wellbeing of the beloved, contrasts very strongly with the behavior of other lovers in *Arcadia*.[4] The quality of Argalus's love, which rises entirely above consideration of beauty or ugliness to love Parthenia for what she is in herself, gives him a moral elevation that no one else can match. Certainly Amphialus, who fell in love with Philoclea when he saw her bathing naked and forces his attentions on her against her will, cannot lay claim to so pure and unselfish a devotion.[5] Yet, by the logic of the events that he has set in motion, he kills Argalus and afterward he kills Parthenia, who, disguised as a knight, challenges him to single combat so that she may die by the same hand that killed her husband. When he finds out what he has done, Amphialus is appalled, as well he may be, for in pursuit of his own gratification he has destroyed living embodiments of human love at its finest. Sunk deep in melancholy as he remembers the shames and mishaps of his life, he takes to his bed. He is roused by a challenge from Musidorus, appearing anonymously, and in the course of this terrible fight he is brought to death's door, escaping with his life only because friends and soldiers sent by Cecropia intervene and carry off his desperately wounded body.

The last scene that Sidney wrote for Amphialus is as moving and full of drama as any. Devastated to discover how the princesses have been treated in his castle while he was incapacitated, he becomes again the unintentional instrument of a death, that of his own mother. At this point all the destructive momentum of his career reaches its culmination and there appears to be nothing left for him but suicide, but first he speaks a terrible elegy on himself, summarizing a career of destruction and disgrace (NA, 441; P, 573).

Sidney's revision of *Arcadia* breaks off soon after this. The story of Amphialus as it stands is one of a good and noble and loving man whose virtues have a canker at their root. When crucial choices have to be made in extreme situations he sacrifices honor and loyalty to the urgent demands of his own desires. The decision causes him shame and anguish, but he cannot rescind it. The consequences it entails appall him, but he cannot bring himself to withdraw from the position he has taken. His is not the tragedy of a malign fate, but full expression is given to the operations of a fatal flaw in an otherwise great and noble character, and what is put before the reader is the logical development of one unhappy event out of another and the torment of a good man who sees himself acting as an agent of evil.[6]

The treatment of Amphialus's character and unhappy career has far-reaching implications in *New Arcadia*, especially in relation to the experience of love. Argalus and Parthenia are the measure of what a truly unselfish love can be, and Argalus, when Parthenia is disfigured, gives a notable example of how love, first evoked by beauty, can become quite independent of outward attractiveness. The love of Amphialus for Philoclea neither rises to this unselfishness nor is refined of its sensuality, but by the standards of Argalus, Pyrocles and Musidorus must also be judged faulty. To consider their conduct against the background of the histories of Argalus and Amphialus is to gain an insight into what Sidney was doing with his interwoven web of characters and how he intended the careers of Pyrocles and Musidorus to be understood. If Argalus is the virtually perfect example of the male lover, but one whose heaven on earth in worldly conditions cannot survive, Amphialus is the flawed example who by his failures creates his own hell. Pyrocles and Musidorus do not reach the purity of Argalus and are subject to the temptations of Amphialus; the interest is in how far they overcome these or succumb to them.

Selfishness and sensuality are threats to the highest ideal of love and the princes are not immune to them, though the emphasis falls differently in each. To Pyrocles the temptation of sensuality is the stronger threat. His defense of love in his early disputation with Musidorus shows a characteristically Sidneyan blend of the wholly admirable, the doubtful and the specious. The course of his reply to the antifeminist attacks of Musidorus, in particular, follows a rather unsteady progression:

> they [women] are capable of virtue: and virtue, you yourself say, is to be loved, and I too, truly. But this I willingly confess, that it likes me much better when I find virtue in a fair lodging than when I am bound to seek it in an ill-favoured creature, like a pearl in a dung-hill. (NA, 73; OA, 21; P, 135)

As for Musidorus's fears that love, which has made him disguise himself as a woman, will make him effeminate in character too, he remarks with nudging emphasis: "I assure you, for all my apparel, there is nothing I desire more fully than to prove myself a man in this enterprise" (NA, 74; OA, 22–23; P, 136).

As the reader encounters them at an early point in both *Old* and *New Arcadia*, these comments of Pyrocles are entertaining and altogether acceptable from a vigorous and ardent young man. But later on, as Sidney builds up his polyptych of lustful lovers, all seeking with more or less rapacity their physical gratification, it becomes apparent that Pyrocles' lighthearted preference for virtue in a fair lodging may lead him into a trap. He is himself, because of his beauty, the focus of unrestrained and illegitimate desire. The aged Basilius uses one daughter as a pander and neglects the elder and heir to his crown, to say nothing of his intended infidelity to his wife, so besotted is he by Zelmane's charms. Gynecia, his queen, abandons a lifetime of virtue, marked by admirable conduct in every sphere, in the grip of uncontrollable desire for Pyrocles. So ravenous and implacable is her appetite that she hates and would be prepared to kill Philoclea, whom she recognizes as her rival. When both girls and the young man are in danger in Amphialus's castle, it is only for Pyrocles' safety that she cares. Because she knows that her passions, in savage pursuit of gratification, are in essence murderous, she does not deny the charge of killing Basilius in the final trial scene, although she is in fact innocent of that. The later developments of the story (existing only in the *Old Arcadia* version) contain a scene in which Pyrocles and Gynecia find themselves together in a cave, and their situations, both wracked by thwarted passion, are perilously similar, although not identical since Pyrocles' is a legitimate and Gynecia's an illegitimate desire (OA, 179–85; P, 632–38). The scene is deeply ironic, for Pyrocles, hearing Gynecia singing of her woes, recognizes the song as an expression of his own feelings, and he goes to greet this sharer of his torments. He finds Gynecia, the last person he would wish to be alone with, and breaks out into a cold sweat "as if she [Pyrocles/Zelmane] had been ready to tread upon a deadly stinging adder." The episode constitutes a crisis in the development of the story, and the momentary equating of Pyrocles' desire for Philoclea with Gynecia's desire for him underlines the dangers of sexual passion. Whether this scene would have been retained in the revision if Sidney had continued his work so far cannot be known, but it would be perfectly consistent with the tendency of the revisions Sidney did make. Both *Old* and *New Arcadia* contain, in fact, an earlier scene that runs closely parallel, with Gynecia and Pyrocles coming upon each other in a lonely spot (NA, 122; OA, 94; P, 216), and here also the dangerous congruity between Pyrocles and Gynecia is manifest.

At the late stage of *Old Arcadia* where it occurs, the encounter with

Gynecia in the cave forces Pyrocles to take drastic measures in an attempt to deal with the whole complicated and dangerous situation. By arranging assignations in the cave with both Gynecia and Basilius he contrives that husband and wife should embrace each other, thus restoring order and propriety in one area. This is a serious point, though Basilius's exit from his lodge to keep what he believes is an illicit appointment is treated as comedy. Father and mother being out of the way, Pyrocles takes the opportunity of going to Philoclea and at last enjoying the full satisfaction of his desires. His plans have no aim but to deal with the immediately pressing demands on him made by Basilius and Gynecia and to satisfy his own balked passion for Philoclea. There comes into his mind as he looks at her lovely body an erotic blazon he had once heard sung, and his sensuous enjoyment of the consummation that follows is frankly stated as Sidney leaves him: "Beginning to envy Argus's thousand eyes and Briareus's hundred hands, fighting against a weak resistance, which did strive to be overcome" (OA, 243). It is in the bedroom that they are seen by Dametas, and Pyrocles' Amazonian deception is revealed.

This scene as it originally stood, and its aftermath, carry through the sexuality motif in the treatment of Pyrocles, but Sidney altered this version of events. In the amendment, though Pyrocles still goes to Philoclea's room, there is no physical consummation of love. Sidney, by this time working on his recasting of the whole work, had evidently come to the conclusion that he had originally allowed Pyrocles to go too far. As he added to his examples of variant sexual relationships and discriminated the different admixtures of pure love and sexual desire, Pyrocles' lovemaking came to seem too coarse an act for the fine sieve that he had created, and he corrected the mistake even before he arrived at the point of rewriting the whole context of the scene. The sensual element in the prince's love remains, but more delicately indicated. The blazon is retained but is now placed in the scene (NA, 190; P, 287) in which Pamela and Philoclea bathe naked in the river while Pyrocles (as Zelmane) looks on. The sight of her beauty has impelled him to run to touch, embrace, and kiss her, but he has controlled himself and confined his attentions to singing of his admiration of her body. As it happens, Amphialus is also a witness of this scene, and at this moment he falls in love with Philoclea. Pyrocles, discovering his presence and angry with him, fights and wounds him. Thus Pyrocles and Amphialus are brought into relation with each other, and their experience is to some extent equated. Yet Amphialus's love will be doomed to despair, and Pyrocles' will eventually reach fruition.

Before considering further the difference in their fates, it will be helpful to take account of Musidorus and the points of similarity between him and Amphialus. It is noticeable, to begin with, that whereas Pyrocles in his guise as Zelmane inflicts one slight wound on Amphialus, Musidorus has two very bloody and near-fatal encounters with him, fought with extreme bitterness on both sides. Pyrocles knows Amphialus as a rival lover, but Musidorus's experience of him occurs only after the abduction of the princesses and he sees him entirely as an abuser of force. The first fight occurs when, at a late stage in the battle between Basilius's and Amphialus's armies, a knight in black armor rides in to the support of Basilius's cause. This is Musidorus, and his efforts turn the advantage to Basilius's side. Amphialus, seeing his prowess, seeks him out and engages him. When the combat seems likely to end soon with the death of one or the other, an old tutor of Amphialus intervenes and the fight is broken off. The second fight occurs at a much later stage, after the deaths of Argalus and Parthenia, when Musidorus's anonymous challenge rouses Amphialus from his state of lethargy and despair. Here again there is no conclusion, but both are severely wounded. On this occasion both men are clad in black armor. Amphialus deliberately rejects his usual armor and trappings to appear all in black; on his shield is a device depicting night and a motto, "From whose I am, banished." Musidorus is more elaborately and symbolically furnished than in his earlier appearance, but still in deepest black. Both men indicate by word and image that they are banished from the sight and favor of the women they love. Musidorus, however, sincerely blames himself and carries a whip in his helmet "to witness a self-punishing repentance," whereas Amphialus's furniture, though it imitates rag-gedness and poverty, is in fact "daintily joined together with precious stones." In this it reflects the ambiguity of his position in relation to Philoclea, "being of the one side a slave and of the other a jailor" (NA, 401; P, 532).

Though Amphialus and Musidorus have never met except in these combats, there has been an earlier episode that linked them, again through the agency of a suit of armor (NA, 57–58; P, 119). Musidorus has come across abandoned armor that he learns belongs to Amphialus and, on a whim, puts it on. The consequence is that he becomes embroiled in a misunderstanding with travelers who take him for Amphialus. It can hardly be doubted that Sidney means to establish some close connection between the two men, and the key to it is the selfishness already discussed in relation to Amphialus and selfishness, in particular, associated with violence.

The reason for Musidorus appearing anonymously at the siege of the castle and in the guise of a banished lover is that, in his last interview with Pamela, he has deeply offended her. After long wooing, she has at last acknowledged that she loves him, whereupon he, seizing a moment when they are alone together, takes her in his arms to kiss her. Pamela, deeply angered at the liberty he takes, dismisses him harshly, a reaction that may, taken by itself, seem disproportionate and even unnatural—but episodes in *New Arcadia* need to be assessed in relation to the whole and the attempted kiss is a matter of greater significance than may at once appear. One aspect of it will be discussed in the next chapter, but the immediately relevant point here is its link with the *Old Arcadia* account of how, while they are eloping together, Musidorus is tempted to ravish Pamela in spite of a vow he has made to her to keep her inviolate until they are married (OA, 202). Sidney altered this passage, as he did the story of Pyrocles' night with Philoclea, and in the emended text no notion of rape is allowed to enter Musidorus's mind. The fact remains, however, that some degree of self-assertion by force, regardless of the girl's will and contrary to his claim to honor and respect her individual rights, is part of the conception of Musidorus's character.[7] That it is part of Amphialus's character is already clear, aggravated in him by the fact that he has unmistakable evidence that he is an unacceptable lover to Philoclea.

Thus it appears that the elements of character that have such disastrous consequences for Amphialus are also present in Pyrocles and Musidorus. These young men are not pasteboard heroes but subject to temptation, weakness, and error, and they do not preserve themselves immaculate in Arcadia. Yet they do not quite fall. Even in *Old Arcadia*, where Pyrocles' behavior steps beyond the bounds Sidney later allows him, he does at least resist the temptation that Gynecia offers. She is beautiful and young enough to be attractive, she does not scruple to titillate his appetite, but susceptible to physical charms as he is, he controls himself out of respect for his love for Philoclea (see, for example, OA, 205; P, 657). In *New Arcadia*, when he and Philoclea are for once alone and have acknowledged their love for each other, he has an opportunity to take advantage of the situation:

"Ah sweet Philoclea," said Pyrocles, "do you think I can think so precious leisure as this well spent in talking? Are your eyes a fit book, think you, to read a tale upon? Is my love quiet enough to be an historian? Dear princess, be gracious unto me."

And then he fain would have remembered to have forgot himself. But she, with a sweetly disobeying grace, desired him that her desire, once for ever, might serve, that no spot might disgrace that love which shortly, she hoped, should be to the world warrantable. Fain he would not have heard, till she threatened anger; and then the poor lover durst not, because he durst not. (NA, 276; P, 375)

That, with its play on "desire" and Pyrocles' acceptance of Philoclea's edict, is a clear indication that in Sidney's second thoughts about Pyrocles he wished to show that the quality of his love was such as enabled him to overcome the temptations implicit in love itself. The little exchange contrasts very tellingly with that later one between Philoclea and Amphialus when she begs him to free her and his other captives and he equivocates: "I find myself most willing to obey you. . . . But alas, that tyrant love . . . will no way suffer it. It is love, it is love, not I which disobey you" (NA, 323; P, 451), and he gives her cause to fear that he means to rape her.

As for Musidorus, when he comes in his black armor to fight Amphialus for the second time carrying the whip "To witness a self-punishing repentance" (NA, 405; P, 536), he continues to accuse himself most bitterly for his disrespectful attempt to take a kiss without Pamela's consent. Amphialus by contrast wears in the crest Philoclea's knives, taken from her against her will, tokens of a "forced favour," and it disgraces him that he should do so. Though he deplores his own violence or condoning of violence, he cannot bring himself to surrender the fruits of it, such as they are.

One further comparison between Amphialus and the princes harks back to the earliest point of his story, the episode from which all his misfortunes and errors flow. Helen, Queen of Corinth, fell in love with him and offered him her heart, but he made no answer and left the court at once. Then followed the death at his hands of Philoxenus and of his father immediately after. He sends a bitter message back to Helen, which she reports to Musidorus as she tells him the whole story. In the letter, Amphialus writes "that he well enough found I [Helen] was the cause of all this mischief, and that if I were a man, he would go over the world to kill me; but bade me assure myself that of all creatures in the world he most hated me" (NA, 65; P, 127). Musidorus in his turn sends a message to Amphialus by his page: "tell him, from an unknown knight who admires his worthiness, that he cannot cast a greater mist over his glory than by being unkind to so excellent a princess as this queen is" (NA, 66; P, 128). How excellent Helen is the reader learns in full in book 2 (NA, 253–54; P, 351–52), when Pyrocles describes her to Philoclea. His reference to Helen and her love for Amphialus occurs in the middle of the story of one of his and Musirodus's adventures before they came to Arcadia, when they were persecuted by the passion—for either or both of them equally—

of Andromana, the queen of Iberia. She imprisons them and will not allow them freedom to leave the country unless they satisfy her desires. The princes were, as Pyrocles reports, "in a great perplexity, restrained to so unworthy a bondage, and yet restrained by love which (I cannot tell how) in noble minds by a certain duty claims an answering" (NA, p.250; P,349). Her love moves them in some degree, but her shamelessness alienates them. They also think of her husband, who has saved their lives. To grant her demands would be "wickedly injurious to him . . . and to accuse a lady that loved us of her love unto us we esteemed almost as dishonourable." Love, it seems, even when unwanted and even when the source is as unworthy as Andromana, is not to be treated with contempt: how much more does a man owe to a woman like Helen. The point is reinforced in the story of the unhappy girl Zelmane, who cannot love the man who loves her but fastens her affections instead on Pyrocles. He treats her and her memory with great tenderness, risking his life to fulfill her dying request to save her father and adopting her name when he takes his Amazonian disguise in Arcadia.

The character of Amphialus is obviously crucial in *New Arcadia*. He generates the totally fresh action of the siege in book 3 of the revised text, but his expansion of the action there, important as it is, is of less significance than his contribution to the panorama of moral choice and judgment that *New Arcadia* brings into view. By creating him as a man of admirable and noble qualities befitting a hero of first magnitude and by locating in him the propensities to sensuality and the improper use of force that are also present in Pyrocles and Musidorus, Sidney clears up whatever ambiguity may attach to the characters of the young princes in *Old Arcadia*.[8] Pyrocles and Musidorus know temptation but do not fall in *New Arcadia*. Amphialus allows Sidney to keep a lightness of touch in dealing with the princes but at the same time to treat the issues of temptation and failure very seriously. To be finely endowed, to nourish high aspirations and benevolent motives, to be young, ardent, and powerful, are situations that can readily, perhaps inevitably do, provide the seed-bed of abuses. Pyrocles and Musidorus are allowed to escape with chastening but not devastating consequences, but Amphialus lives out the results of succumbing to the weaknesses that might have overwhelmed the other two. His creation is an extraordinary achievement. As an element in the intellectual economy of the book, his character is brilliantly conceived; as a figure in his own right, he claims interest, admiration, and sympathy and stands as a tragic figure doomed to destroy by uncontrolled impulses all that is noblest and best in him. Yet his career is evidently not designed to be ultimately tragic. Though very near to death at his last appearance in *New Arcadia*, he is not dead, having failed to kill himself outright by falling on his sword and stabbing himself with Philoclea's knives. The long-suffering and deeply loving Queen Helen comes to take him to Corinth, where lives the doctor who once effected the miraculous cure that restored Parthenia to her beauty. A new and better life seems likely to be in store for Amphialus when, freed of the errors that blighted him, he learns to value and accept the love he once rejected and all his gifts are directed into healthier channels. In addition to its other functions, the character of Amphialus has this other very important one: it illustrates the humanity, the charity, and the warmth of fellow feeling with which Sidney watches the efforts of his characters to walk the dangerous razor edge of the good life. Failure may be redeemed, sin may be forgiven: this attitude informs *Arcadia* in all its versions, whether the lightly handled original text or *New Arcadia*, which works out more fully and with greater clarity what was sketched and sometimes insufficiently delineated in the earlier version.

Recognition of the technique of comparison and contrast, as Sidney applies it to his male characters in the revised *Arcadia*, is essential in order fully to understand how he meant them and the actions they are engaged in to be viewed. Its application is widespread, and only some major examples have been selected in this chapter. It is equally essential in consideration of his women characters, for Sidney adopts the same procedure with them. He uses it with the same care and the same subtlety, and there is a corresponding enhancement of meaning in all that is involved. It is in reference to the women that *Astrophil and Stella* has a special contribution to make to appreciation of *Arcadia*, and the next chapter will take up this point, as a preliminary to closer focus on the treatment of the women of *New Arcadia*.

2
Stella and the Growth of the Heroine

Chronologically Sidney's sonnet sequence, *Astrophil and Stella*, comes between the completion of *Old Arcadia* and Sidney's increasingly concentrated work on the revision. It is predominantly concerned with the experience of the male lover, Astrophil, and does not overtly encourage the reader to give much attention to Stella. There is, nevertheless, an undercurrent of interest in her that deserves to be brought to the surface, in particular for its importance as a contribution to the development of *New Arcadia*.

A straightforward description of *Astrophil and Stella* runs something like this: the sequence deals with a young man's experience of love, and it touches on all the themes present in love poetry at least from the *stil novisti* onward. Love as carnal appetite, love as aspiration to ideal beauty, love as devil-provoked illusion, love as an intimation of the divine—all are here, together with discussion of the role of reason and the teachings of philosophy and religion. The treatment of this complex of themes is sharpened by its setting in a particular environment at a particular time and with reference to an individual life. The setting is a late-sixteenth-century court where the courtiers gossip about love affairs and also about the political situation at home and abroad. The life is that of a young man of promise whose family and friends expect great things of him. The core of the sequence is the tracing of the impact of love upon this young man as it changes, for better or worse, the perspective in which he views his own previous interests and the assumptions of his society. At first he resists the experience but is drawn more and more completely into it. When he finds at length that his pursuit of the beloved is hopeless, he emerges once more into the outer world and resumes his career, though bearing with him the marks of his experience. This story—the word is appropriate—is told with remarkable vivacity in an equally remarkable variety of styles and moods. It includes dramatic scenes (sometimes complete with dialogue), debate, lyric celebration or protest, wit that can be comic, tender, or cynical, and both high-mindedness and sophisticated coarseness.

This description is in terms of Astrophil's experience, and being so it identifies *Astrophil and Stella* firmly with the sonnet tradition. "It is Petrarch, more than Laura, who is the centre of the *Rime*," J. H. Whitfield writes. The main interest of the poems, he continues, is provided by "the conflict generated within the mind of Petrarch. To it doubtless Laura is essential, but it is, to use a language Dante might have used, as accident to substance."[1] What is true of Petrarch is true of others. A recent book, *The Metaphysics of Love*,[2] details the arguments, the conflicts, and the accommodations provoked by theory and experience, but the woman implied in the relationships is participant only to the extent that she is to be reacted to, and as an individual she gets no attention. This is, incidentally, a gap that Christina Rossetti tried to fill in her sonnet sequence *Monna Innominata*, but deep as her sensibility was, it took its coloring from nineteenth-century England and hardly helps to illuminate the nameless and silent ladies of the past. Castiglione's courtiers, indeed, raised the question "whether women be not as meete for heavenlie love as men";[3] but the debate was deferred to another time—which never came.

Sidney need not, however, have accepted the tradition unreservedly. Certainly he had studied Petrarch, but he was not in the business of mere imitation, of Petrarch or anyone else. He had also admired *Troilus and Criseyde* and may have drawn inspiration from Chaucer for his own treatment of disappointed love—Chaucer gave a good deal of sympathetic attention to Criseyde; but, whatever the influences, it is clear that Sidney meant his own version to be an up-to-date one, modern in feeling and background. Petrarch's long-deceased woes do not bind him, and neither does Stella's role need to be patterned on Laura's or governed by the same restraints. Nevertheless in the early sonnets it looks as though she may be destined to be just one more "uninterested and uninteresting girl,"[4] among the number whom Petrarchizing poets made the object of their poetic loves. At this stage Astrophil is very well aware of the claims of the world outside, its demands and its opinions, and aware also of himself as bright young man and poet, engaged in recording his emotional and intellectual waverings. It is not until sonnet 31 that the reader first glimpses Stella herself, in the famous poem addressed to the moon ("With how sad steps, o Moone, thou climb'st the skies"), the ostensible point of which is to accuse Stella of "ungratefulness" because she makes no response to his wooing. This, admittedly, does nothing at all to individualize her, but in sonnet 36 she is put in action, to the extent that Astrophil hears her sing, and in sonnet 40 she moves much more fully into the focus of attention as her lover addresses her directly:

O Stella deare, how much thy power hath wrought.

From this point on, the external world recedes, and Stella, becoming the center of Astrophil's preoccupation, acquires some degree of identity, even if still only as reflected through him. He bemoans her unresponsiveness but sees her moved by a story of unhappy lovers—Sidney may be hinting at Dante's tale of Paolo and Francesca in *Inferno*, canto 5, in which a reading of the story of Launcelot and Guenevere becomes an incitement to adultery. The irresistible power of her presence breaks down Astrophil's resolution to leave her, and the sight of her at a tournament unnerves his arm. The conflict that had first been an internal one, fought out in Astrophil's own mind between reason and passion, now becomes a duel, between Stella's virtue—that is, her chastity—and Astrophil's desire, inflamed by the beauty of her appearance. Recognizing the conflict in these terms, Astrophil becomes quite brazen about what he wants, and at this point Stella finally emerges from the shadows and becomes an active agent in the affair. In sonnet 62 she tells Astrophil that she loves him.

This is a confession that the living Laura withheld from Petrarch, though she confessed it after death: no. 302 of the *Rime* hints at it, and in *The Triumph of Death* Laura appears in a vision, to explain her whole treatment of her lover, meting out to him alternate encouragement and discouragement as a discipline of love. Stella's poet does not credit her with the same control of the situation, but he ascribes to her similar intentions. Laura denied Petrarch her love in her lifetime so that he might not dishonor both himself and her, and Stella, though she acknowledges love for Astrophil, is not to be thought of as sanctioning an adulterous relationship. She loves "a Love not blind," and she wills Astrophil to fly the "tempests of vain love" and anchor himself on virtue's shore. Like Laura, she has care for her lover's well-being, though in her case it is his worldly career she is thinking of, not his spiritual destiny. She adduces all the arguments that in the earlier stages he had himself acknowledged, but now he is too far gone in his passion for her to find any force in them. "No more, my deare, no more these counsels trie," he begs her. Appeals to ambition, of whatever kind, cannot move him:

"Thou art my Wit, and thou my Vertue art"

(64)

A crisis is precipitated when she allows him to kiss her, and emboldened by this, he urges her too far. "Full of desire, emptie of wit," (82), he frightens her. When they meet he expects consummation, but now she sees that a stop must be put to the affair, though it hurts her as it hurts him. "Tyrant honour" (Eighth song), not some more sublime concept, impels her, and fear of disgrace and shame. Evidently she does not escape unscathed as it is (93), and in their last interview (Eleventh Song) fear stifles any expression of affection she might feel.

There is a story of Stella, then, as there is of Astrophil, that of a young woman moved at last by her wooer to make a response, endeavoring to keep the relationship on a chaste footing but persuaded by his importunity to allow a kiss and finding that she has inflamed him to almost uncontrollable ardor. She restrains him gently for his own good, but Sidney, with a notable realism, does not leave things on a note of pure renunciation. He sites his story in a real world of jealous husbands and scandal, and after the delicacy of the two meetings described in songs 4 and 8, prudential considerations take over and Stella's story ends in fear:

> Come no more, least I get anger.
>
> (xi)

The beloved woman, we may say, is taking shape and assuming a character with reactions, conflicts, hopes, and fears of her own, as *Astrophil and Stella* progresses. It is not an heroic character, but it is lifelike. Stella belongs to her background as Astrophil does to his, and feels its different pressures equally: this is a drama for two, not one. For both it ends in frustration. The two poems from *Certain Sonnets* that used to be printed at the end of *Astrophil and Stella*, "Thou blind man's marke" and "Leave me o Love," were never suitably placed there, for to neither party does renunciation appear as a salutary discipline on the way to moral or spiritual enlightenment. George Watson has commented on "how little the spiritualising side of Petrarch's genius appealed to the Elizabethans"[5] and Sidney is no exception to this generalization.

The picture of courtly love in the sequence is probing and realistic, but it was not enough for Sidney. *New Arcadia* is evidence that he wished to go deeper into the questions raised by sexual relationships, questions he had handled dramatically but not profoundly in the sonnets. He had been brooding over them for some time, and *Astrophil and Stella* represents, in effect, the second stage of his thinking, the first being *Old Arcadia*. In the early version of the romance, the stranger-shepherd Philisides figures prominently as a young man lamenting his unhappy love for his "star"; the connection with *Astrophil and Stella* is obvious. A second clear link is that a debate about the worthiness of love takes place early on in *Old Arcadia*, making much the same points as in the early sonnets of the sequence. In *Old Arcadia* it has the additional edge that Musidorus, the elder of the two princes who has not yet succumbed to the charms of the princess Pamela, is extremely scathing about the nature of women. To love and respect them, he believes, is to derogate humiliatingly from the dignity of manhood. In his later work on *Arcadia* Sidney wished to eliminate Philisides almost, if not quite, entirely, for his thinking had by then moved out of the confines of a single immediate situation to a wider consideration of the potentialities, for good or evil, of love. The debate between the princes and Musidorus's virulent criticism of women are retained, but the role of the heroines is very much built up and one result of this is that Musidorus has to undergo a painful penance and learn better. That there is a continuous line of thought running throughout these three works, recognition of which enhances the reading of each of them, can be illustrated by a telling example of the treatment of common material. The illustration comes from epi-sodes involving kissing, the *baiser*, a topic on which Ronsard in particular, but not alone, lavished much attention. The kiss focused much of the ambiguity that so worried and fascinated thinkers about secular love. Some *baisers* are most luxuriantly sensual, but at the same time it was possible for Castiglione to describe the kiss as "a coupling of soules" rather than of bodies and an act perfectly per-missible to chaste lovers.[6] No wonder that Stella, in Sidney's se-quence, was confused, and no wonder either that Sidney sees the taking or giving of a kiss as a moment of great significance.

Toward the end of book 1 of *Old Arcadia*, Musidorus rescues Pamela from attack by a bear. She meantime has fainted with fear, and before she comes to, "Softly taking her in his arms, he took the advantage to kiss and rekiss her a hundred times" (OA, 52). Later, when she is again unconscious, asleep this time, he intends to go further "and see whether at that season he could win the bulwark before timely help might come" (OA, 202). The scene of intended rape recalls the second song of *Astrophil and Stella*. Astrophil finds Stella sleeping and sees his chance:

> Her tongue waking still refuseth,
> Giving frankly niggard No:
> Now will I attempt to know
> What No her tongue sleeping useth.
> See the hand which waking gardeth,
> Sleeping, grants a free resort:

> Now I will invade the fort;
> Cowards *Love* with losse rewardeth.

But Astrophil, when it comes to the point, unlike *Old Arcadia*'s Musidorus, dare not. Fear of "her just and high disdaine" restrains him, and he contents himself with stealing a kiss. Stella, aware of the liberty he takes, is at first angry but afterward forgives him, unwisely as it turns out.

In *New Arcadia* Musidorus takes no kisses when Pamela faints, nor does he attempt to take advantage of her when asleep, but a significance in both episodes that is not brought out at all in *Old Arcadia* and is no more than faintly suggested in *Astrophil and Stella* is given strong emphasis in the revised version. When Pamela at last accepts Musidorus and he takes her in his arms to kiss her "as it were, to establish a trophy of his victory" (NA, 309; P, 436) to his amazement, he is met with just that "high disdain" which Astrophil fears in the second song if he attempts to force the sleeping Stella. Musidorus's act in attempting to kiss Pamela without first obtaining her consent is much less heinous, and Pamela's fiercely offended reaction may seem absurd. It is to be taken seriously, however, for the episode marks the final stage of Sidney's progressive emancipation of women from their role as merely objects of sexual desire whose feelings and responses are to be taken for granted. What Astrophil dimly perceives in the second song is enforced upon Musidorus with great severity, and he has to learn that Pamela is an individual whose selfhood and personal dignity are at all times to be respected.

The point is echoed in relation to the other pair of young lovers in *New Arcadia*. Pyrocles, full of joy when he finds his love requited, wants at once to consummate it, but Philoclea restrains him: "Love showed himself a cowardly boy, that durst not attempt for fear of offending," Sidney writes, and then adds a correction: "But rather Love proved himself valiant, that durst with the sword of reverent duty gainstand the force of so many enraged desires" (NA, 234; P, 337). Pyrocles, on this and on other occasions, "found it a great war to keepe that peace" but "so she absolutely badde him, and he durst not know how to disobey" (NA, 258–59; P, 357).

In Pyrocles Sidney emphasizes the sensual aspects of male love, in Musidorus the aggressive and the dominating. Both are taught better by their princesses, but the young women also have lessons to learn. Philoclea has to develop some courage and firmness of character to supplement her sweetness, and Pamela has to learn softness of feeling to temper her high-heartedness. Both the heroes and the heroines grow into love and face problems in their experience of it. Stella of the sonnets also grows into love, but the sequence lacks a resolution. Stella has neither the authority that Laura claims to minister to her love's well-being nor the depth and strength of character that Pamela and Philoclea in their several ways develop. She is not strong enough to help toward a resolution of her and Astrophil's dilemma. A married woman, she is anxious to preserve her honor, but she weakens so far as to allow Astrophil some liberties, then takes fright and turns him away. Developing her side of the story, Sidney seems to have come to envisage that the role of the woman could be the crucial point in the whole debate about love. It could bypass the old conflict between reason and passion, for if the woman were really worthy, a fully developed and acknowledged person in her own right who commanded the genuine respect of her lover, then love would be, not what Iago said it was, and Musidorus in his unenlightened state believed, a "lust of the flesh and permission of the will," but an experience that could only enhance the virtue of good men and women. In the particular situation of *Astrophil and Stella*, Stella's marriage is the insuperable bar to fulfillment of love, but Sidney is from the beginning less concerned with that as a moral issue than with more general questions about love itself, and it is these that he consistently probes in the sonnets. The character of the woman comes, as his thinking develops, to be seen as the pivotal issue. She needs to be available for marriage, of course, as Stella was not, but more importantly, she needs to have a free-standing strength and integrity. Stella, for one reason or another, lacks these, and the experience of the love affair remains for this reason unproductive either of physical satisfaction or moral enlargement.

For Spenser, in the *Amoretti* sequence, the desires of the flesh and the love of woman are sanctified by God:

> . . . let us love, deare love, lyke as we ought,
> love is the lesson which the Lord us taught

and his love poetry is permeated by religious reference. *Astrophil and Stella,* however, is a secular sequence. There is an ironic reference in sonnet 5 to Cupid as "that good God" whose worship makes church and churchmen starve, but otherwise reason and passion, virtue and love, fight things out on a secular field. The same is true of *Arcadia,* whose action in both versions is pre-Christian. The tone deepens in the later developments of the story as Sidney goes further into political, moral, and religious questions, but he keeps it all on the far side of Christianity. In sequence and romance alike he examines love as human experience, with its deceptions, weaknesses, and follies but also its aspirations and its capacity for refining and exalting. Astrophil and Stella fail to make much of the experience, though Astrophil, at least, refuses to reject it. Sidney himself continued to work at its problems and found a way to resolution by building up the character of the beloved in the remarkable portraits of Pamela and Philoclea in *New Arcadia;* but these young women are not *donne angelicate,* for they are credibly and fallibly human and subject to correction on their own account. *Old Arcadia, Astrophil and Stella,* and *New Arcadia* are all parts of a continuous exploration by Sidney of aspects of human behavior, particularly sexual love, a subject he clearly saw as related to the deepest and furthest ranging issues. The evidence of his life shows him to have been a deeply religious man, but in his original work he kept his feet on the ground and his sense of humor alert. He wrote of men and, increasingly, of women, dealing subtly and penetratingly with moral questions and touching with delicacy and restraint on the spiritual life. His imaginative work provided him with a way to enquire without irreverence into the basis of his faith by studying the strengths and limitations of human nature as it is in and by itself. The interest he expressed, even on his deathbed, in pagan philosophy witnesses to the same desire to gather and assess all the evidence possible about human capacity, for through this he seems to have hoped to grasp more firmly the relation of man to God. Human capacity, whether for good or ill, includes the capacity of women, and *Astrophil and Stella* shows Sidney's developing interest in this theme. The conclusion must be that the portrayal of female characters in *New Arcadia* should be studied with care, and the next chapter will offer evidence of how worthwhile such attention may be.

3
Sidney and the Characters of Women

C.S. Lewis wrote of the princesses Pamela and Philoclea that "They can be praised without reservation. English literature had seen no women to compare with them since Chaucer's Crisseid; and, apart from Shakespeare, was to wait centuries for their equals."[1] John Danby also praised the characterization of the princesses and made a good critical point in reference to them: "Sidney's discriminations are finer than we have been in the habit of making for three hundred years."[2] To engage in discrimination is to take characters and their moral stature seriously, and Sidney prepares the way for his extensive studies of female natures by placing near the beginning of *Arcadia* a justification of so much and so careful attention to subjects by no means inevitably found worthy of it.

Very early in *Arcadia*, Pyrocles confesses to Musidorus that he has fallen in love, and Musidorus is horrified at the news. Implicated in the debate that follows about the nature of love is a crucial question concerning the nature of women. Musidorus, who has not yet seen Pamela and who scorns the state of being a lover, attempts to shame Pyrocles out of his passion by reminding him that he is a *man* and that to partake of anything "womanish" is to be disgraced. Pyrocles has adopted a female disguise, in itself shameful, and risks adopting female characteristics too. "'You must resolve,' Musidorus tells him, 'if you will play your part to any purpose, whatsoever peevish imperfections are in that sex, to soften your heart to receive them'" (NA, 71; OA, 19; P, 133). Pyrocles in his reply defends love, and claims that it is compatible with virtue, but first he defends women and has evidently given his arguments some thought: "'I am not yet come,' he says 'to that degree of wisdom to think light of the sex of whom I have my life, since if I be anything . . . I was, to come to it, born of a woman and nursed of a woman.'" Men by "their tyrannous ambition," he goes on, "have brought the others' virtuous patience under them" and, not content to have done so, then insult them with "unmanlike cruelty." Reason should teach that women "are framed of nature with the same parts of the mind for the exercise of virtue as we are. . . . And truly, we men and praisers of men should remember that if we have such excellencies, it is reason to think them excellent creatures of whom we are, since a kite never brought forth a good flying hawk" (NA, 72–73; OA, 21; P, 135).

Musidorus, when he sees Pamela, recants, and to make the reversal of his views all the more striking, Sidney comments, in *Old Arcadia*, "that he was wounded with more sudden violence of love than ever Pyrocles was" (OA, 41), the agonies he suffers being perhaps, Sidney suggests, love's revenge on him for "the bitter words he had used." The point that retribution is exacted remains the same in *New Arcadia* but is developed with greater finesse. The characters of the princesses have larger room to develop in the revised text, and by an irony that Sidney must have planned with amusement, the girl who wins Musidorus's heart gives ample evidence of her majesty of demeanor and her "high heart." Pyrocles, who praises women's capacity for Amazonian valor, loves the shy and gentle Philoclea, but Musidorus, who dispraises their idle hearts and weak hands, falls at the feet of one who, even when she returns his love, insists that he treat her with the most punctilious respect. His humiliation and remorse following his attempt to kiss her are evidently a punishment for his masculine arrogance and insensitivity in earlier days.

In the *New Arcadia* version of their adventures, Pyrocles and Musidorus arrive at different times in Arcadia, having been shipwrecked on their way to Greece and separately rescued. Musidorus gets there first and is given hospitality by a noble lord, Kalander. Among other amenities of Kalander's splendid mansion is a room full of pictures, including a large painting of Basilius, ruler of Arcadia, his wife, Gynecia, and their younger daughter, Philoclea—Pamela, the elder, is not with them. The picture rouses Musidorus's curiosity, and Kalander obligingly gives him (and the reader) an account of the state of affairs in the country. Together with this brief history, Kalander also gives Musidorus thumbnail sketches of the women of Basilius's family. Gynecia he describes as beautiful and intelligent "and in truth of more princely virtues than her husband . . . but of so working a mind and so vehement spirits as a man may say it was happy she took a good course, for otherwise it would have been terrible" (NA, 16; P, 76). His account of Pamela and Philoclea balances and compares: "more sweetness in Philoclea but more majesty in Pamela . . . love played in Philoclea's eyes and threatened in Pamela's . . . Philoclea so bashful . . . so humble . . . Pamela of high thoughts, who avoids not pride with not knowing her excellencies, but by making that one of her excellencies to be void of pride; her mother's wisdom, greatness, nobility but . . . knit with a more constant temper." Having introduced the royal ladies by way of the painting, Sidney turns from them to set in motion the stories of other women whose lives will to some degree interlock with theirs and, more importantly, whose experiences will contribute to rounding out the world of feminine action and choice as *New Arcadia* presents it. Parthenia is a type of womanly excellence as Argalus is of manly, and her story before her marriage anticipates aspects of the later story of Philoclea. Like Philoclea persecuted by the unwelcome love of Amphialus, she is importuned by Demagoras, a man who loved "nobody but himself and, for his own delight's sake Parthenia" (NA, 28; P, 88). Parthenia's mother favors his suit, and as Cecropia torments Philoclea and Pamela, so Parthenia's mother, "witty and hard-hearted," does all she can to break Parthenia's spirit. She employs Argalus in dangerous enterprises, in the hope that he will be killed, but his valor is equal to all trials and, similarly, "to Parthenia, malice sooner ceased than her unchanged patience." Despairing of success, Demagoras resorts to "unmerciful force," the smearing of the poisoned ointment that ruins her beauty, and the story then develops as has already been described. As Argalus stands to the male characters in the book, so stands Parthenia to the female, giving an example of unimpugnable excellence. She is obedient to her mother until she meets Argalus, and then, knowing what love is, she refuses Demagoras firmly, though with sympathy for the pain she must inflict. She endures patiently all the ill treatment that follows at the hands of her mother, and when her beauty is lost she thinks only of Argalus's welfare not her own, just as he, in the crisis, rises above all selfish feeling and cares only for her.

The marriage of Argalus and Parthenia is the immediate prelude to the first signs of Pyrocles' falling in love, but the development of this situation is deferred while the story of Helen, Queen of Corinth, intervenes. She is unhappily in love with Amphialus, and her love story is again a triangular one, the unwanted suitor being this time Amphialus's friend and foster-brother Philoxenus. Philoxenus is no villain like Demagoras, but, equally, Amphialus is no paragon like Argalus. Neither is Helen as faultless as Parthenia. She confesses that before she knew Amphialus, her heart was "utterly void" of affection, "as then esteeming myself born to rule and thinking foul scorn willingly to submit myself to be ruled" (NA, 60; P, 122). When she falls in love, she retains still some hardness of heart. Unlike Parthenia, who treats the unworthy Demagoras with consideration, Helen is indifferent to the feelings of the amiable Philoxenus and makes a cruel response to his offer of love. With more thought and care her on part, the fight that takes place between the friends, and that results in the deaths of Philoxenus and his father, might never have occurred. The blood then shed marks both Helen and Amphialus.

Helen's behavior shows a culpable pride and selfishness and evidently contrasts strongly with that of Parthenia. Both she and Amphialus fail to make an adequate response to love, she in her unfeeling dismissal of Philoxenus, he in his bitter repudiation of her, and the result is suffering and long estrangement. During this time, Amphialus's pursuit of Philoclea leads to the kidnapping and the bloody siege, but for Helen it is a period of penitential pilgrimage. She has come to a different understanding of what love is and requires and has learned to temper pride with penitence and patience. Sidney thereafter speaks of her with respect and admiration, as indeed he does of her behavior before Philoxenus wooed her and brought Amphialus to help him in his suit. Her failure to rise to the demands of that situation is the one blemish in an admirable life, but its consequences bring great unhappiness. Fulke Greville tells us that Amphialus and Helen were to marry at the end,[3] and this must be assumed to have been Sidney's intention since Amphialus, though desperately wounded in body and mind, is not actually dead after his suicide attempt and Helen arrives to take him to Corinth to be healed. We do not know how, on the other side of near death and nursed back to life by Helen, Amphialus would have voiced his experience. The reader does know that *she* has come a long way from her first arrogant queenliness to her lament over Amphialus's barely living body: "Alas, why should not my faith to thee cover my other defects, who only sought to make my crown thy footstool, myself thy servant?" (NA, 444; P, 577). Her love and self-abnegation save him from the destructive path of self-will on which he was set. Clearly the contrast in their responses to unrequited love is a major point of their stories as Helen emerges out of initial selfishness to become a major force of regeneration through love selflessly offered.

The story of Parthenia's love for Argalus shows that gentleness like Philoclea's does not preclude dignity, courage, and resolution when inspired by a fitting love: these are qualities that Philoclea will acquire as she matures during *New Arcadia*. The story of Helen, on the other hand, strikes a more cautionary note, for she is born to rule, like Pamela who is her father's heir, and pride in herself and her position is nearly her undoing. As Amphialus channels off the worst consequences that might follow from incipient weaknesses in the princes, so does Helen in respect of Pamela.

It is after the stories of Argalus and Parthenia and Helen and

Amphialus have been set in motion that the princes' debate about
love takes place. Read in the context that Sidney provides, the
theoretical oppositions gain animation, for the ambivalence of love,
which has the power to inspire and ennoble but also power to degrade
and destroy, has been illustrated in what has been narrated. Musidorus's misogynism has not, however, been given any backing, for
both Parthenia and Helen are noble women. Nor will Musidorus's
insults be heard again.[4]

There is soon to follow, however, an example of womanly behavior
to set against the virtues of Parthenia and Helen. Kalander remarked
that it would be terrible if a woman of Gynecia's intelligence and
strength of character should take bad ways, and that "terrible" even-
tuality comes to pass as she conceives a violent passion for Pyrocles.
Sidney's treatment of Gynecia is one of the most remarkable pieces of
characterization in *Arcadia*, particularly so because of the liberal attitude he takes toward her.[5] It is already striking in *Old Arcadia* and
becomes more so in the revision, because of the enlarged context in
which she is set. He endows her with two traits that may be guaranteed in most periods to rouse male prejudice, but far from Sidney
castigating her as a monster, he treats her with understanding and
sympathy. In the first place, Gynecia is a strong-minded woman and,
potentially, at any rate, a dominant one. Sidney refused to believe
that this is necessarily a bad thing. When later he describes Queen
Andromana, he presents her as another formidable woman who "had
made herself so absolute a master of her husband's mind that a while
he would not, and after, he could not, tell how to govern without
being governed by her . . . entrusting to her the entire conduct of all
his royal affairs" (NA, 248; P, 347). Sidney's comment on this may be
unexpected: "A thing that may luckily fall out to him that hath the
blessing to match with some heroical-minded lady." His wife's su-
premacy is not, in fact, a blessing to the King of Iberia, and he does
not deserve that it should be, but Sidney's point stands nevertheless.

Gynecia and Andromana share another trait, the second on which
male judgment often bears hard: they are both not only sexually eager
but also sexually aggressive. Both are married to much older men, and
both conceive an ungovernable passion for a younger one. Both
become shameless in their demands and the means they employ to try
to seduce the young men, and both use threats when persuasion fails.
But Andromana has a history of adultery and unscrupulous sexual
exploitation behind her (NA, 215–22; P, 312–20), whereas Gynecia is
"of most unspotted chastity" (NA, 16; P, 76) until she is overcome by
her passion for Pyrocles. She has a conscience that inflicts its terrors
upon her at every stage: " 'Forlorn creature that I am,' she exclaims in

the cave, 'I would I might be freely wicked, since wickedness doth prevail; but the footsteps of my overtrodden virtue lie still as bitter accusations unto me' " (OA, 183; P, 635). She is about to reach the lowest point of her decline, invoking the aid of "infernal furies" to "assuage the sweltering of my hellish longing"—though nothing can appease her guilty conscience—and when Zelmane comes upon her unexpectedly, her desperate passions are unleashed in threats against Pyrocles himself and against Philoclea too unless he satisfies her passion. Even at that point, when she most nearly speaks the language of melodrama, she cannot but acknowledge her own sense of guilt.

Gynecia sins against her better nature, and in the end she repents most feelingly, but Sidney creates her as a real woman, not simply as a moral exemplum. She was very young when married to Basilius, and he was already an old man. Sidney encourages obvious deductions about repression of natural instincts and desires and allows the reader to watch with sympathy the flaring up of repressed fires in a woman of early middle age who sees life passing her by. Her jealousy of her daughter, though in one sense unnatural, is in another a perfectly natural growth out of the situation: "the growing of my daughter seems the decay of myself," Gynecia comments (NA, 279; OA, 122; P, 378). Sidney understands all this as well as a modern psychologist and is ready to show compassion to Gynecia, but he does not forget the wrong she is doing to Basilius. A hint dropped apparently casually is more effective than fulminations against rampant sexuality would have been. Gynecia, enduring her usual tormented conflict of passion and conscience, has a restless night and disturbs Basilius from his sleep. He "took her in his arms and began to comfort her, the good man thinking it was all for a jealous love of him; which humour if she would a little have maintained, perchance it might have weakened his new-conceived fancies" (NA, 224–25; OA, 113; P, 322). She makes no response, however, and this chance to deflect him from his ridiculous passion for Pyrocles in his Amazon garb is lost. Basilius is a very foolish old man but not essentially a bad one, and the little scene shows how his heart is penetrable by pity and affection. Gynecia might have saved him from pursuing his folly to serious lengths if she had had any regard for him at this moment. As it is, they leave each other to cherish their misbegotten loves and to plot adultery with increasing shamelessness.

Gynecia repents but Sidney does not claim that the desire that Pyrocles has aroused dissolves away as though it had never been. In her first horror, as Basilius falls apparently dead before her and she believes that just retribution has come upon her, even then, remembering Pyrocles, she knows that she still loves him (OA, 280; P, 730). In prison as she awaits trial and execution, she is torn between hatred of him as the cause of her downfall and love that had still "a high authority in her passions" (OA, 364; P, 799), and at the trial itself she dare not look at Pyrocles' face "for the fear these motions in the short time of her life should be revived which she had with the passage of infinite sorrows mortified" (OA, 376; P, 898) The imaginative empathy that Sidney shows in all this enables him to keep clear without any confusion the moral status of the different phases of Gynecia's story and yet to avoid simplifications that would misrepresent the real nature of individual experience. Such treatment of women like Gynecia may be rare at any time; in the 1580s its care, subtlety, and understanding are almost beyond belief.

The character of Gynecia belongs to the first conception of *Arcadia* and is not materially altered or much enlarged in *New Arcadia*. Response to her is affected, however, and recognition of the subtlety of Sidney's treatment of her enhanced, by his use of the favored technique by which he seeks to illuminate the understanding of his characters in *New Arcadia*—that is, the development of another figure to pair with her and make possible those moral discriminations which are so large a part of the dynamic of the revised text. Cecropia, mother of Amphialus, occupies to some extent more familiar literary ground than Gynecia, for she stands in a long line of wicked women, ambitious, cruel, and godless. Yet even here there are touches that endow her with individuality. She has wit, as in her responses to Amphialus when she first breaks the news of the kidnapping of the princesses. She can adopt a smooth, insinuating tone when she judges there is profit in it (see her attempted persuasion of Philoclea in *New Arcadia*, book 3 (NA, 330–33; P, 457–62), and she loves her son, though her influence on him is always evil. There is a world of difference between her and Gynecia, though both for considerable stretches of the plot are acting as wicked women. Cecropia's is a settled and, with one exception, cold-hearted wickedness. Gynecia's is an aberration, psychologically accounted for and plausible, which triumphs temporarily in the face of her own never-entirely-overcome resistance and which is repented and atoned for. Cecropia dies in the agony of believing Amphialus dead by his own hand and ordering, as a last act of malice, the murder of the princesses: "but everybody seeing (and glad to see) her end, had left obedience to her tyranny" (NA, 440; P, 373)—whereas Gynecia, having passed through agonies of shame and penitence, will live to be once more highly honored and to observe for the rest of her life "all duty and faith to the example and glory of Greece" (OA, 416; P, 847)

The moral standing of Sidney's characters is always defined against a wide range of alternatives, and the teasing out of tangled skeins of virtue and vice requires careful discrimination. The more delicate the discriminations, the more convincing—"life-like" is C. S. Lewis's word—the result will be. So Andromana is lustful like Gynecia and calculating like Cecropia, but Gynecia has the conscience that the other two lack, and Cecropia knows no passion but ambition and has experienced no love, except for the son whom she regards as an extension of herself. The presence of the others illuminates and gives extra life to each, and the system of comparisons and contrasts of which they are a part provides the background for the presentation of Pamela and Philoclea.

Pamela, the elder daughter and Basilius's heir, is proud and has a "high heart." She is full of disdain at the arrangement by which Dametas, the herdsman, is her guardian, and there is no question of her countenancing Musidorus's suit until she has received his assurance that he is a prince by birth and a worthy match for her. In this she is avoiding the error of Erona, princess and later queen of Lycia, who gives her love to a young man of mean parentage and pays dearly for so doing. Even after she has heard and believed Musidorus's account of his parentage, Pamela is hardly won, feeling that she owes it to herself to remain aloof and even cold, rather than seem in any degree oncoming. Musidorus has to humble himself and exercise great persistence in his services and set out his personal qualities very fully before she will allow herself to relent toward him. Sidney, in fact, greatly heightens Pamela's reserve and dignity in *New Arcadia*, as, for example, in the different handling of the scene in which Musidorus communicates to her, under guise of recounting someone else's story, the facts of his princely birth and present disguise as a shepherd (NA, 134–41; OA, 103–8; P, 227–34). Pride is a keynote of Pamela's character, a quality not improper in her as heir to the throne, but similar high position led Helen of Corinth to unbecoming lengths. Self-respect that demands a high standard of self-control in herself and in her lover is also a proper quality but may degenerate into mere self-regard without due consideration for another. Helen is guilty of that in her treatment of Philoxenus but she repents. A coarser-grained example is Artesia, a young woman brought up by Cecropia and trained in her way of thinking, so that she believed "she did wrong to her beauty if she were not proud of it, called her disdain of him [her wooer] chastity, and placed her honour in little setting by his honouring her" (NA, 91; P, 154). She has resolved never to marry "but him whom she thought worthy of her and that was one in whom all worthiness were harboured"—which makes her sound very like Pamela. Evidently, in Pamela's virtues there are dangers of real, not only assumed, coldness, of arrogance, and of vanity. It is relevant that Cecropia diagnoses vanity as a potential weak point when she notes how carefully Pamela has dressed herself during her imprisonment in Amphialus's castle.

Lewis describes the characterization of the princesses as both idealized and lifelike. Both words are justified, but Sidney's conception is deeper than either suggests. Pamela's virtue exists and is maintained, like that of the princes, in the equilibrium created by opposite tensions. Around her are displayed various kinds of imbalance that result when characteristics similar to her own are not sufficiently disciplined, and it becomes evident that the exercise of moral judgment is being continuously called for in response to the different kinds of pressure that are put upon her. As needs always to be said about Sidney's characters, Pamela is much more than a moral exemplum. Severe as she may be, she is also very human. She cannot resist talking to her sister about the accomplishments of the new shepherd, Dorus (Musidorus), and does it in a style so far from her usual collected manner that Philoclea guesses the secret of her love immediately. When she has angrily dismissed Musidorus from her sight because of the stolen kiss and he writes to her, she treats the letter at first "as if it had been a contagious garment of an infected person, and yet was not long away but that she wished she had read it, though she were loath to read it" (NA, 310–11; P, 438). A touch of hypocrisy enables her to succumb: "At last she concluded it were not much amiss to look it over, that she might out of his words pick some further quarrel against him."[6]

A more serious and moving moment occurs at the end of Pamela's noble prayer when, alone and at the mercy of enemies, she kneels to offer to God her patience under suffering and asks for strength to endure whatever may be in store for her. Her prayer ends with a plea that the wickedness of those who persecute her may never prevail upon her purity of mind and body and then she pauses: "'And, O most gracious Lord,' said she, 'whatever become of me, preserve the virtuous Musidorus'" (NA, 335–56; P, 464). Throughout her captivity it is of him that she thinks more than of herself, and the thought of him makes her falter a little in accepting what seems like inevitable destiny. "'Since the world will not have us,' she says to Philoclea, 'let it lose us. Only,' (with that she stayed a little and sighed) 'only my Philoclea' (then she bowed down and whispered in her ear) 'only Musidorus, my shepherd, comes between me and death, and makes me think I should not die, because I know he would not I should die'" (NA, 451; P, 580).

Pamela, then, proud, high-hearted as she is, is as capable of tender and devoted love as Parthenia and Helen. Nor is she frigid, if the *Old Arcadia* account of her elopement with Musidorus is to be relied upon. She binds him to preserve her chastity until they can be married, but she herself feels the temptation of their proximity and the congenial opportunity: "her travailing fancies . . . had bound themselves to a greater restraint than they could without much pain well endure" (OA, 198; P, 650). Sidney might have made further modifications in this episode in the course of rewriting, but *Old Arcadia* shows her enjoying a "virtuous wantonness" (OA, 200; P, 652), and it is clear that he does not want her to be thought cold. She is, as Kalander has said, like her mother in many ways but "knit with a more constant temper" (NA, 17; P, 76). Her love for Musidorus is not to be underestimated because of the restraint under which, unlike her mother, she keeps her passion.

If the strength of her character presents some dangers and temptations to Pamela, it is her gentleness and lack of self-assertion that may constitute a threat to Philoclea, both in relation to the situations she has to meet in the course of the story and in terms of the author's success in engaging interest in her. Sweet, bashful, and humble are words applied to her by Kalander, and however attractive they may be, they do not seem to promise much in the way of dramatic interest. Sidney is careful to give the assurance, when describing Parthenia, that her quietness, modesty, and lack of assertion are not the result of an empty mind, but to the contrary. She has "a most fair mind; full of wit" (NA, 28; P, 88), but Philoclea may be only a charming and rather characterless child. The child, however, is compelled to grow up, and Sidney sets himself deliberately to chart the process in a passage introduced by a rare first-person intrusion. The author as "I" and his first audience as "fair ladies" make frequent appearances in *Old Arcadia*, but authorial distance from the narrative is preserved in *New Arcadia*. When it breaks down at this point it signals the presence of a particularly delicate piece of analysis (NA, 143–46; P, 237–40).[7] *Arcadia* is very largely about sex and the impact of sexual passion, but Philoclea, when the story opens, is too young to know what sex is. She learns in circumstances that might be expected to be extremely damaging. She finds herself strongly drawn to the young Amazon, Zelmane, who has so surprisingly penetrated Basilius's forest retreat and been accepted into the royal household. She sees her father besotted by the stranger and her mother also obsessed by her, and she finds herself drawn step by step into a state of emotional turmoil. She believes the Amazon is really the woman she appears to be, and the sexual desires that now begin to haunt her imagination night and day appear to be hopeless of fulfillment. From innocence she has entered into experience, and the results are restlessness, vain longing, and a gamut of emotions. She begins to understand what her mother feels and her mother's passions seem to legitimate hers—a dangerous deduction, as the wording of her soliloquy underlines. Thinking of her apparently unnatural passion, she exclaims: "Sin must be the mother and shame the daughter of my affection" (NA, 149; P, 243). Her language becomes more unrestrained: "Do I not see my mother as well, at least as furiously as myself, love Zelmane, and should I be wiser than my mother?" The answer, of course, should be "yes," but for the young Philoclea, used to obedience to her parents and quite unaccustomed to making an independent judgment, there is a real possibility that she might model herself on Gynecia. Her final words in the scene, however, show that the break has been made. Philoclea is no longer the child of her parents but the woman who gives herself to her lover: " 'Oh my Zelmane,' she says, 'govern and direct me, for I am wholly given over unto thee.' "

The clearing up of her confusion about the nature of her love for Zelmane/Pyrocles comes soon after, when Pyrocles has at last the opportunity to declare his real identity. The tangle of Philoclea's emotions is unraveled by the discovery that the seeming Amazon is a man, but that happy result emerges out of a situation that itself indicates what it means to pass from sexual innocence to experience of a passion that welcomes subterfuge and is content to accept un-seemly facts so long as they remain unspoken. Basilius employs his daughter to intercede in his favor with Zelmane, and Philoclea ac-cepts the commission gladly, since it gives her the opportunity to talk to Zelmane alone; but the pleasure is bought at the cost of knowing beyond doubt that her father seeks to make Zelmane his mistress and is using her for an immoral purpose. Her joy when Zelmane reveals herself to be, in fact, a man is likewise shot through with some shame, for she fears that she has not maintained the entire reserve and modesty by which, her upbringing tells her, she should keep a suitor at arm's length—and that her sister practices. Yet she frankly avows her love and, giving her heart to Pyrocles, entrusts her honor to his keeping. She was recently childlike and unknowing but has become thoughtful and dignified: "Thou hast then the victory; use it with virtue. Thy virtue won me; with virtue preserve me. Dost thou love me? Keep me then still worthy to be beloved" (NA, 233; OA, 121; P, 330). Philoclea's sweetness has its own kind of strength as she emerges into adult life, a point made more strongly in *New Arcadia*. Hers is not the militant pride of Pamela, but she compels obedience all the same, requiring of Pyrocles a new kind of valor in controlling his "enraged desires."

There is much that is charming in the love scene of Pyrocles and Philoclea in the *New Arcadia* version, and sense of its quality and of the nature of the participants is enlarged by aspects of the stories that Pyrocles goes on to tell at Philoclea's request. One of the first of these concerns a man called Pamphilus—young, handsome, of noble blood, a delightful and accomplished companion, but a seducer and betrayer of women. His skill lies in playing on the weaknesses of his victims, jealousy, envy, vanity, pride. He discards them without compunction when he grows tired of them and triumphs over their misery with insults. Pyrocles encounters him at a crucial moment, when the betrayed women have banded together to take revenge on him, and he hears the whole tale from the most determined of the avengers. It is a story that cuts two ways, Pamphilus is what Pyrocles might become if he chooses to exploit his attractions without care or respect for the women who are charmed by him; and the fate of the women enforces the need for that circumspection and restraint toward love which Philoclea reproaches herself for having to some degree failed in. Pamphilus does wrong, but in doing so, he takes advantage of his victims' faults.[8]

Sidney, characteristically, makes Pyrocles' informant (with tongue in cheek he christened her Dido) capable of a shrewd piece of self-analysis: "'I must confess,' she says, 'even in the greatest tempest of my judgement was I never driven to think him excellent, and yet so could set my mind both to get and keep him, as though therein had lain my felicity: like them I have seen play at the ball grow extremely earnest who should have the ball, and yet everyone knew it was but a ball'" (NA, 238; P, 336). What rankles particularly with Dido is that Pamphilus has insulted her beauty, claiming that he could find many fairer than she, an interesting point because female vanity is one of many topics on which Sidney does not follow the conventional line.[9] It plays little part in the characters of any of the beautiful women to whom he gives his attention. The tournament in book 1 of *New Arcadia* in which knightly lovers are challenged to assert their ladies' preeminence in beauty gives Sidney the opportunity to find the mind's construction in a range of women's faces (NA, 94–105; P, 157–68). His portraits are as much psychological as physical and in many cases serve as introductions to characters to be seen in action later. Though Gynecia and Philoclea both have their champions in this tournament and their knights are overthrown, their defeat causes the women little disturbance. Gynecia, the reader is told, would have been quite indifferent to the downfall of her defender at any other time and only cares at all now because Zelmane is a witness. Philoclea, whose softer nature might be more receptive to flattery, reacts to the defeat of her champion only to the extent of "a pretty blush" denoting "a modest discontent." As for Pamela, Cecropia believes that her care for her appearance during her imprisonment denotes vanity, but she is shortly disabused in no uncertain way. Feminine susceptibility to vanity is given some prominence only in the person of Dido, whose story, together with that of her fellow victims, shows what may happen when women allow themselves to be cajoled and flattered into trusting men without honor—their hearts will be broken, their fortunes lost, their reputations ruined. Philoclea's confiding herself to Pyrocles might be a rash act, but looking back to her after reading the Dido story, her confession of love can be recognized as something heroic rather than foolish, which calls for and receives a fitting and honorable response.

If some potentialities in Philoclea's nature are revealed by Dido and her companions, she is set off in quite another way by the girl whose name Pyrocles takes when he adopts his Amazonian disguise, Zelmane. Zelmane has fallen in love with Pyrocles during an earlier adventure outside Arcadia. She has the double misfortune to be the daughter of Plexirtus, a man of unremittingly wicked disposition, and to be brought up by the lustful and unprincipled Andromana. In spite of these evil influences, she is herself good and is loved by Palladius, Andromana's son. Like Zelmane, he is the virtuous child of a wicked parent, but this community of fortune is not enough to bind Zelmane to him. She employs him, however, to help Pyrocles and Musidorus escape from Andromana's clutches, and as a result of this he is killed, to the distress of the princes. Some time later Pyrocles and Musidorus are joined by a youth who begs to be taken into Pyrocles' service. Though he has an idea that the boy's face is familiar, Pyrocles does not recognize that "he" is in fact Zelmane, who follows and serves him devotedly, her eyes full of the love she dare not acknowledge and that he does not recognize. By Plexirtus's villainy, Tydeus and Telenor, knightly brothers with whom Pyrocles and Musidorus feel some affinity, are killed, and out of shame for her father, and grief that Pyrocles' hatred of him will turn him against her whenever he discovers her identity, Zelmane pines away. As she dies she reveals herself, begging Pyrocles to think of her tenderly: "'this breaking of my heart, before I would discover my pain, will make you, I hope, think I was not altogether unmodest'" (NA, 267; P, 366). "Was not this love indeed?" is Viola's comment on her supposed sister's story in *Twelfth Night,* and the story of Zelmane, as Sidney tells it, is also a touching little tale. Pyrocles himself is much moved by it, and it has a great influence on both princes and on Philoclea. Zelmane and Philoclea physically resemble each other, a fact that contributes to Pyrocles' falling in love with her when he first sees her portrait. Pyrocles has adopted Zelmane's name in Arcadia, and earlier, in response to Zelmane's dying request, he called himself Daiphantus, the name Zelmane took when she served as his page. Musidorus, also by her wish, went by the name of Palladius, Zelmane's unhappy lover. Palladius and Zelmane loved without requital and sacrificed themselves for those they loved. They are examples of the selflessness of true love, as are Argalus and Parthenia, and the use of their names serves to keep their example before the eyes of the young men in their own amorous pursuits. Zelmane cuts off her hair and strives to appear boyish, subjecting herself, though a princess, to a servitor's role, and Pyrocles also disguises his sex and accepts embarrassment and disability for the sake of the girl he loves. The patient courage and humility that Zelmane displays become part also of Philoclea's education in what love will demand, and how well she learns her lesson is to be seen in book 3 of the *New Arcadia*. Gentle and malleable as she has been, she proves that she can resist torment and tyranny with courage and fortitude despite the natural softness of her nature. "With silence and patience" she bears what Cecropia and her assistants inflict on her, comforting and sustaining herself with thoughts of Pyrocles: "that was the only worldly thing whereon Philoclea rested her mind, that she knew she should die beloved of Zelmane, and should die rather than be false to Zelmane . . . easing the pain of her mind with thinking of another's pain, and almost forgetting the pain of her body through the pain of her mind" (NA, 421; P, 553).

When Cecropia threatens to kill Pamela, Philoclea is able to rise to the height of magnanimity and offer her own life to save that of her sister and friend, and when Pyrocles urges her to give Amphialus some appearance of hope in his suit, in order to gain time, she rejects his plea with quiet resolution: "Trouble me not, . . . dear Pyrocles, nor double not my death by tormenting my resolution. Since I canot live with thee, I will die for thee." In words that recall Zelmane's, she begs that after her death he will love her memory. Zelmane knew, sadly, that he would one day love another as he had not loved her, but Philoclea asks to be his last love. " 'Remember,' she says, 'that my love was a worthy love' " (NA, 430; P, 562), and by this time she has earned the right to make this claim.

One further touch relating to Philoclea's character is worth noting. It occurs in the later part of the story and appears, therefore, only in

the unrevised text. As it stands, it forms part of a little group of
episodes that are clearly meant to illuminate each other by comparison. This is the technique that Sidney employs extensively in his
filling out of the narrative in *New Arcadia*, and he could quite suitably
have retained at least the main elements in a final revision. The
episodes concern the reactions of three women when they find, or
believe they find, that they have been spurned and betrayed by a
man. The first is Gynecia in the scene in which she and Pyrocles
encounter one another in the cave. Pyrocles at first attempts to fend
her off by maintaining his pretence of being a woman, and Gynecia
bursts out in rage, scattering threats in all directions: "Since I must
fall, I will press down some others with my ruins. Since I must burn,
my spiteful neighbours shall feel of my fire. . . . Believe it, believe it,
unkind creature, I will end my miseries with a notable example of
revenge" (OA, 184; P, 637). This episode is followed by an account of
Musidorus's plots to get Dametas and his family out of the way, so
that he and Pamela can make their escape. His story to Miso,
Dametas's misshapen and witchlike wife, is that her husband has
taken up with a very pretty young shepherdess and has an assignation
with her that night in the neighboring town. Miso's anger and jealousy are unbounded: "her hollow eyes yielded such wretched looks as
one might well think Pluto at that time might have had her soul very
good cheap. But when the fire of spite had fully caught hold of all her
inward parts, whosoever would have seen the picture of Alecto, or
with what manner of countenance Medea killed her own children,
needed but take Miso for the full satisfaction of that point of his
knowledge" (OA, 192; P, 645). The reference to Pluto should probably serve as a reminder that Gynecia in the previous scene, despairing of her virtue, had invoked the furies to assist her in satisfying her
desires. The reference to Medea must certainly recall that among
Gynecia's threats is one that "that accursed cradle of mine [i.e.,
Philoclea] shall feel the smart of my wound." Gynecia's soul, like
Miso's, seems at that point to be on offer "very good cheap." Sidney's
juxtaposition of the serious-passionate and the comic-grotesque is a
striking example of the two-toned effect that enhances so much of
Arcadia and by which the reader is amused and entertained even
while, simultaneously, the intellect and the moral sense are challenged and invigorated. In this instance the juxtaposition functions to
lighten the tone and to discharge some of the horrifying potential in
what Gynecia has said. She has been driven to her lowest point, and
as her words indicate, the possibility of a fearsome tragic outcome
looms distinctly on the horizon. Miso's jealous frenzy acts as an
effective counterweight and reassurance that all will be well. At the

same time, it exposes an element of the ridiculous in jealousy itself and the actions it leads to. The double nature of jealousy, deadly and yet absurd, has been a rich subject of drama, developed with particularly acute appreciation of both the terror and the nonsense in *Othello*. Sidney's narrative sequence is more leisurely and has a different end in view, but the temporary equation of Gynecia and Miso is a daring device and effective in setting out some parts of one of the most tangled complexes of human feeling.

After Gynecia and Miso comes Philoclea. In pursuit of his plan to gain time by holding out hope of satisfaction to both Gynecia and Basilius, Pyrocles has to appear cold to Philoclea and completely discontinue all the attention he has previously paid to her. Philoclea, ignorant of his plans, is desolated by the sudden, studied indifference. She feels herself to be abandoned both by her parents and by her lover and suffers intensely. In this condition, "she had yielded up her soul to be a prey of sorrow and unkindness, not with raging conceit of revenge—as had passed through the stout and wise heart of her mother—but with a kindly meekness taking upon her the weight of her own woes, and suffering them to have so full a course as it did exceedingly weaken the state of her body" (OA, 214; P, 668). Philoclea's behavior, as the woman (apparently) scorned, reflects her mild and humble nature, as distinct from the strong and, what Sidney ironically calls, the "wise" heart of her mother, and from the termagant violence of Miso. Philoclea does not so much renounce revenge as never contemplate it, but her quiet suffering speaks for itself and her reproaches when they come are all the more pointed and bitter in their effect because of the sweetness of the nature that has been so injured. In this episode again, Sidney is at pains to show that Philoclea, though constitutionally gentle, is not a feeble or insipid character. The depth and sincerity of her love give her strength to defy death and also to accuse her lover when she believes he has betrayed her. "Humble-hearted" whereas Pamela is "high-hearted," she has her own kind of strength, and Sidney's success in creating her is a triumph in a very difficult undertaking, achieved by great delicacy of idea and treatment.

Sidney has evidently devoted much care to the delineating of his range of female characters, and the thought and skill bestowed on them are matched by the generosity and enlightenment of his attitudes. He disregards conventional judgments and rejects stereotypes, creating both good and bad women who are strong minded and intelligent and allowing to even the more timid and pliable Philoclea a growth into conscious self-respect, courage, and resolution. Which is the more remarkable—the sustained double portrait of two kinds of virtue in Pamela and Philoclea, or his analysis of Gynecia, standing so close as she does to the violent, implacable female figures of old stories and yet sympathetically distinguished from them—it is hard to say; but given skill of this kind, and attitudes of this kind, it is surely rash to make conventional assumptions about the implications of Pyrocles' female disguise. Musidorus, before he learns to love and respect Pamela, is in no doubt that Pyrocles' Amazonian masquerade is a disgrace, and recent commentary has been inclined to accept this.[10] A man's adopting of a female disguise has traditionally been looked on as an act of degradation that would invite real as well as apparent diminishment of his male status, but it does not follow that Sidney would share the traditional view. The degree and kind of attention he pays to his women characters seems, on the contrary, to point in a quite opposite direction. The jewel that fastens Pyrocles' mantle is carved to represent Hercules with a distaff in his hand, as he was when Omphale set him spinning among her maids, and its motto is "Never more valiant." Sidney might perhaps have intended the motto as an ironic comment, and in conventional commentary on the Hercules episode it could hardly be anything else; but, in fact, the words can be taken quite literally in relation to Pyrocles.[11] Though his tone may be equivocal when he assures Musidorus that "for all my apparel, there is nothing I desire more than fully to prove myself a man in this enterprise" (NA, 74; OA, 22–23; P, 136), there is no ambiguity in Sidney's comment on his response when Anaxius's brother, Zoilus, tries to embrace, as he thinks, the Amazon Zelmane: "abiding no longer abode in the matter, she that had not put off (though she had disguised) Pyrocles, being far fuller of strong nimbleness, tripped up his feet so that he fell down at hers" (NA, 460; P, 590). If any doubt remains that Pyrocles may have weakened either in strength or courage, the ensuing fight with Anaxius must remove it.[12] When he lays aside his princely rank and disguises his sex, exposing himself to unfamiliar and unforeseeable adventures for the sake of wooing in very unpropitious circumstances the young girl with whom he has fallen in love, Pyrocles takes great risks and makes himself very vulnerable. He suffers dangers and indignities but never, even when on trial for his life, regrets the sacrifice he makes for love or weakens in his devotion to Philoclea. It can be quite fitting for him to claim valor in this conduct, for heroism is not confined to deeds of arms alone.

In his woman's dress Pyrocles has to share something of women's experience, enduring the courtship of unwelcome suitors, practicing patience, and in Amphialus's castle, forced to wait helplessly while others fight and attempt a rescue from outside. In the early debate with Musidorus, he defends the cause of women verbally and, when the opportunity comes, in the episode on which Sidney was working just before he broke off his revision, he fights physically under their colors to punish one who has despised and insulted them. Anaxius is the transgressor, and Sidney draws attention to the significance of Pyrocles' role in chastising him when he makes the young prince forecast that Anaxius will find himself defeated in that martial skill of which he is most proud, and "punished by the weak sex which thou most contemnest" (NA, 465; P, 594). This is not strictly true, of course, but the episode seems clearly intended to have symbolic value as Pyrocles fights as a woman on behalf of women. The whole course of *Arcadia*, in the revision especially, makes claims for the special strengths of women and undermines a masculine pride based merely on muscular power, just as it challenges also male claims to superior virtue. Anaxius, who relies on physical prowess, is to be chastened, as is Musidorus, who despised the character of women and has to do penance, reduced from prince to unskillful shepherd, and bound by Pamela to a most dutiful respect. Rather than derogating from his manhood, Pyrocles' living for a time and in part a woman's life completes it. Sidney describes him as "the chief of the princes," and the reference is not only to his public status but also to his wider range of sympathy and response than that of Musidorus who is limited by a harder masculinity. [13]

The original *Arcadia* was written for Sidney's "dear lady and sister," the young Countess of Pembroke. The dedication is full of affection and betokens an intimate and confiding relationship. It is appropriate that, in working out more fully ideas and themes only sketched in *Old Arcadia*, Sidney should have expanded and enhanced his treatment of women and their claims as individuals to mind, conscience, and character. Lady Pembroke was herself a woman of character and learning who shared her brother's interests and after his death sought to promote them. She was a poet who translated Petrarch and completed the verse translation of the Psalms that Sidney had begun. She assumed his role as a patron of poets and enlisted some (Thomas Kyd among them) in an attempt to refine and elevate English drama. Sidney, writing in the very early 1580s, had seen no way forward but to adopt the patterns and rules of neoclassical drama, and the Countess persisted in this idea even after new impulses were opening far wider horizons. She misjudged in this, but the motivation was what Sidney's had been in his *Apology for Poetry*, that is, to encourage English writers to create a modern literature of comparable dignity and accomplishment to that of Italy and France. Sidney's sister is known by her own work and the praise others gave her. His mother is a more secluded figure, but she came of a great family, the Dudleys, and was evidently a woman of character and intelligence. She nursed the Queen during an attack of small-pox and contracted the disease herself. After that, she avoided appearances at court, "the mischance of sickness having cast such a kind of veil over her excellent beauty," Fulke Greville writes, "as the modesty of that sex doth many times upon their native and heroical spirits."[14] He seems to imply that Lady Sidney herself was of "heroical" mold. With two such women among his most intimate relations, if for no other reason, Sidney had every incentive to treat women and women's experience with respect.

As for Fulke Greville himself, his nature was of a grimmer stamp than his friend's. He acknowledges that women have claims to equality of treatment, but he grounds them on characteristically different premises. In his *Life of Sidney*, he writes of the role of the powerful and wicked women in his plays. "That women are predominant," he explains, "is not for malice, or ill talent to their sex; but as poets figured the virtues to be women, and all nations call them by feminine names, so have I described malice, craft and such-like vices in the persons of shrews, to shew that many of them are of that nature, even as we are, I mean strong in weakness." He goes on to say that he has not made them all evil, any more than all good, but "mixed of such sorts as we find both them, and ourselves."[15] In the work of Samuel Daniel, a younger man closely connected with the Sidney-Greville-Pembroke circle, the sympathetic treatment of women is a particularly striking feature. His Cleopatra, in the French-Senecan play he wrote about her, is a feeling, even tender, woman; his Octavia, reproaching Antony for his desertion of her in a verse epistle, speaks on behalf of all women frustrated by the restraints upon their freedom and confined within "this prison of ourselves"; the verse epistles he wrote in his own person to women recipients are among his most successful poems, expressing much that is best in his mind and character. In the late *Hymen's Triumph* (1615), an Arcadian pastoral play, he comes close to Sidney, when Palaemon reproaches Thyrsis for his weakness in pining for "a silly woman" and provokes a firm counterstatement. The later lines of Thyrsis's speech are an example of Daniel's own remarkable sensitivity:

> And doe you hold it weaknesse then to love?
> And love so excellent a miracle
> As is a woman! ah then let mee
> Still be so weake, still let me love and pine
> In contemplation of that cleane, cleare soule

That made mine see that nothing in the world
Is so supreamely beautiful as it.
Thinke not it was those colours white and red
Laid but on flesh, that could affect me so.
But something else, which thought holds under locke
And hath no key of words to open it.
They are the smallest peeces of the minde
That passe this narrow organ of the voyce.
The great remaine behinde in that vast orbe
Of th' apprehension, and are never borne.

(ll, 1276–90)[16]

The sentiments are very close to those of Pyrocles. The passage may
be an expansion, in particular, of his words in the *Old Arcadia* version
of the scene in which he avows to Musidorus that he has become a
lover: " 'and yet such a one am I,' said he, 'and in such extremity as
no man can feel but myself, nor no man believe; since no man could
ever taste the hundredth part of that which lies in the inwardmost part
of my soul' " (OA, 17).[17]

Sidney himself may have drawn inspiration for his treatment of
women characters from Chaucer's *Troilus and Criseyde*. He singled out
this poem for praise in his *Apology for Poetry*, and being the man he
was, he is likely to have taken note of how much more sympathetically than others Chaucer treats the "sliding courage" of Criseyde.
That he in his turn influenced the thinking of Greville and Daniel, his
ideas taking color from their own individual temperaments, seems so
likely as to be virtually certain. The influence of *Arcadia* did not need
to depend on the reader's personal association with the writer, however. Shakespeare was responsive to Sidney's great romance, and
there is good reason to suppose that the line of splendid Shake-
spearean heroines owes more than an occasional specific reminiscence
to the attitudes and imaginative perceptions that go into the making
of Sidney's remarkable portrayals of the women of *Arcadia*. Desde-
mona with her quiet courage, Cordelia with her high but loving heart,
and Hermione with her dignity and self-respect would recognize first
cousins in *New Arcadia*.

4
Telling the Tales

Not least among the revised *Arcadia*'s claims on the interest of a modern reader is Sidney's own evident fascination with narrative techniques and the whole enterprise of storytelling. Each of the three books has its own characteristics, and together they compose a remarkable display of penetrating critical intelligence and executive virtuosity. Book 1 is largely prospective, book 2 retrospective, and book 3 deals with climactic events and presents them to the reader as they happen. To demonstrate Sidney's interests and the range of his accomplishments it will be most convenient to discuss each book in turn.

(i)

The prospective quality of book 1 can only be properly appreciated when the whole revision, as far as it goes, has been assimilated, for Sidney handles the earlier episodes in such a way that their full meaning and implications become apparent only in the light of information made available at later points. This information is often released fragmentarily, by installments, so that we grow into understanding as we penetrate further into the Arcadian world. Incidents and details that appeared complete enough in themselves when first encountered are likely to turn out to have much more to them than had been thought, with the result that to read the book again is to have a different experience of it. The episode of Pyrocles falling in love with Philoclea's picture is a convenient example of the technique. In *Old Arcadia* Pyrocles is walking with Kerxenus (Kalander in *New Arcadia*) in the gallery of his house when he sees a painting of Basilius and his wife and younger daughter. Pyrocles, attracted by Philoclea's appearance, asks his host for her story, and when he hears of Basilius's retreat to the woods and Philoclea's "strange kind of captivity" to keep her from marriage, he first pities her and then is smitten by love. That the hero should fall in love with a portrait at first sight seems a typical romance episode, to be swallowed as a story-book invention and not taken in any way seriously. Later, however, in *New Arcadia* it transpires that one piece of information was missing from the first account of the episode, and when it is eventually divulged it puts the matter in a different light. Soon after his sight of the picture, Pyrocles disappears, and Musidorus, having searched widely for him, decides at last to return to Arcadia, wondering if the clue to his friend's unaccountable behavior may lie in the picture, which "resembling her he had once loved, might perhaps awake again that sleeping passion" (NA, 68; P, 130). It turns out that Musidorus is right, but what lies behind the reference is not discovered until, in book 2, Pyrocles tells Philoclea the story of Zelmane and her unhappy love: "something there was which, when I saw a picture of yours, brought again her figure into my remembrance, and made my heart as apt to receive the wound, as the power of your beauty with unresistable force to pierce" (NA, 268; P, 367). The threading of this small sequence into the complex narrative tissue of *New Arcadia* is a striking piece of authorial management and illuminates on a relatively small scale what goes on everywhere with large and small narrative units in the book. It illustrates also a characteristic Sidneyan way of dealing with romance episodes and motifs. Falling in love with a picture is *not* to be taken, ultimately, as just the sort of improbable thing a story-book hero would do, but we discover that there was a preparation for it in his earlier history, and the event becomes psychologically credible, deepening our sense of Pyrocles as a character. Sidney makes both him and Musidorus a few years older in *New Arcadia* than they were in *Old Arcadia*. They have gained some greater maturity through the many adventures they have undergone before arriving in Arcadia, and Pyrocles at least, in his relations with Zelmane, has known grief. Only gradually is it revealed what Pyrocles' experience really was when he first saw Philoclea's picture, and with that knowledge the richness of the book is enhanced.

Sidney devises his story in terms of romance materials, but he is not interested in marvels. There is, in fact, one monster in *New Arcadia*, but even that is not impossible to nature (NA, 270; P, 369).[1] Usually the reader is taken behind the scenes and shown how what may appear to be the product of pure fantasy really came to develop out of a chain of credible events. This constitutes, in effect, a variation on the epic formula of beginning *in medias res*. *New Arcadia* opens with the immediate aftermath of a shipwreck and reserves the prehistory to be recounted in the main in book 2. This is a major application of the old narrative formula, but the first shipwreck scene itself provides a

further example of Sidney's distinctive technique, by which he provides, after the event, a quasi-naturalistic explanation of an occur-
rence that may initially appear to have been introduced merely for a
striking effect.

When Strephon, Claius, and Musidorus put to sea in search of
Pyrocles dead or alive, they catch sight of him sitting astride the mast
of a wrecked ship. He is "holding his head up full of unmoved
majesty" and holding aloft his sword, "which often he waved about
his crown as though he would threaten the world in that extremity"
(NA, 8; P, 66). This is a very romantic picture and gives a striking
entry for the young hero, but we find later that it is not only that.
Pyrocles' waving his sword was no mere gesture but had the purely
practical and sensible purpose of drawing attention to himself so that
he might be seen and rescued (NA, 46; P, 107). The sword and its
various uses figure prominently in all the accounts of the shipwreck
(occurring at NA, 7, 46, and 275; P, 66, 107, and 374). Again an
apparently simple, even simpleminded, reference in book 1 opens
out and reveals a deeper perspective than is at first suspected. The
controlled imaginative energy that foresees it all and releases its
disclosures at determined points is remarkable.[2]

Episodes in book 1 depend for their full value, then, on a past
history that comes to light only by degrees as the whole story unfolds,
but other things in book 1 take their point from what is going to
happen in the future, not from what has happened in the past. Both
kinds belong, of course, to the future of the reader as he or she
progresses through the book. Kalander's description of Gynecia is a
case in point (NA, 16; P, 76). He makes it in the course of his
commentary on the painting of the royal family, which so captures
Pyrocles' interest, but this is not the only picture in Kalander's
summer house. "There was Diana when Actaeon saw her
bathing. . . . In another table was Atalanta. . . . Besides many more,
as of Helena, Omphale, Iole . . ." (NA, 15; P, 74). The list may
seem entirely conventional, a numbering of well-known legendary
heroines with perhaps a half-mocking smile at similar mythological
gatherings assembled according to hackneyed literary custom on nu-
merous occasions. This is not in itself unlikely, since Sidney is very
"modern" in his awareness of the act of writing and the role of the
author, as when he describes the "fair field" near Basilius's lodge and
adds that round about it there "grew such sort of trees as either
excellency of fruit, stateliness of growth, continual greenness, or
poetical fancies, have made at any time famous" (NA, 111; OA, 46;
P, 175). But with hindsight it becomes apparent that the identity of
the figures in Kalander's pictures is not merely a roll call of familiar

names. Diana, the huntress, cherishes her chastity and punishes Actaeon for his invasion of her maiden reserve; Helen of Troy brought ruin to men and a city by the beauty that inflamed male desire; for love of Omphale, Hercules took to women's garb and women's occupations, and Iole's love led to his destruction; Atalanta was proud and self-sufficient until she lost her freedom through the guile of a cunning suitor. Women are seen in these pictures as images of chastity and provokers of lust, vulnerable to the snares laid for them by men and also sources of mortal danger to the lovers who become enthralled by them. Pyrocles is to adopt female guise like Hercules, but deceptive appearance plays its part in more than one of these stories and has no simple moral value. The anticipatory function of Kalander's pictures, in any case, goes further than this. It is against the background they provide and the stories they embody that the portrait of Basilius, Gynecia, and Philoclea is introduced, and with the knowledge of the later developments of their story it can be seen how the furnishing of Kalander's gallery raises all the questions relating to the experience of love that the book will fully explore later. Since the men are observers, the questions take the form of examples of women's nature and men's response, for good or ill, to them; how dangerous, physically and morally, will pursuit of love be to the young heroes, Pyrocles and Musidorus? As the work develops, Sidney will show the other side of the situation too and enter carefully and sympathetically into Gynecia's and Philoclea's and Pamela's experience, as their temperament inclines them to one or more of the archetypal roles of Diana, Helen, Omphale, and Iole. In the end, each makes her own accommodation to her female sexuality, and Kalander's garden may indicate of what kind that will be. Before taking us indoors to see the paintings, Sidney describes the garden, among the features of which is a fine fountain depicting a naked Venus giving suck to the young Aeneas. At this fount of benign and virtuous love, the great hero will be nourished and strengthened for his life to come, even if, for a while, as the description suggests, he neglects the true source of nourishment for other attractions: "At her breast she had her babe Aeneas, who seemed, having begun to suck, to leave that to look upon her fair eyes which smiled at the babe's folly, meanwhile the breast running" (NA, 14; P, 74). Book 1 of *New Arcadia* is an extraordinarily careful piece of writing in which scarcely a detail is without its place in the whole composition. The life-giving Venus who smiles at her babe's folly has a significance that carries throughout *New Arcadia*. Virtuous love is beautiful, as the statue of Venus is beautiful. It is patient with its "children's" follies, and its life-feeding flow does not dry up.

The pictures in Kalander's gallery are minor details in themselves, but it is altogether consistent with the methods of *New Arcadia* that attention directed toward them for a moment should have the effect of bringing into view the whole wide context in which they stand. Both *Old Arcadia* and *New Arcadia* have love as their central subject matter, although *New Arcadia* introduces a very much larger political element, but the scope and depth of treatment of the theme are immensely enlarged in the revised version.

The premonitory nature of details such as this and other examples discussed above illustrates the microscopic care and the intellectual concentration that went into the rewriting of *Arcadia*. Larger units in book 1 also serve to prophesy developments to come later and, these developments being known, to illuminate them. The point can be underlined by citing an example where later illumination is missing and its absence is much felt. *New Arcadia* opens with the laments of the shepherds Strephon and Claius over the departure of Urania, their beloved, from the shores of Greece. As Katherine Duncan-Jones has pointed out,[3] there are puzzling features in this episode, especially considered in relation to appearances of the three characters in *Old Arcadia* and the poem added in the 1593 edition (not, of course, added by Sidney) that describes the game of barley-break in which they all participate (P, 197–212).[4] Reading *New Arcadia* is an imitation of life in that the reader learns by experience, later knowledge making sense of what earlier was only partially understood or not understood at all, and that being so, the absence of the ending is a great handicap in attempting to interpret the opening. It is clear that the relations between Urania, Claius, and Strephon exist on a different plane from those of other lovers in the book. Urania "is not essentially a woman at all," Katherine Duncan-Jones writes, and goes on to suggest that she is Venus Urania—as Plato described her, "the noble, the heavenly love which is associated with the heavenly muse, Urania." Certainly she is more than mortal, and just as her significance may have grown out of and supplanted other meanings that appear to be present in cryptic form in *Old Arcadia*, so it might have developed yet further to lead, at the end of the whole work, to some presage of the quality of Christian love.[5]

However this may be, the friendship of Strephon and Claius, so prominent in the early pages, undoubtedly introduces a theme to which Sidney gives serious consideration. The shepherds offer an example that others do not at once reach, if indeed they ever do, for not only are they good men in themselves but also, though they are devoted to the same beloved, their friendship is unimpaired by this. They have had a vision that so elevates and refines them that they are loving to each other without rivalry or enmity and they act with compassion, charity, and delicacy to Musidorus, who is cast up, a stranger, on the shore where they stand recalling the departure of Urania. The sea bore her away and the sea carries him in, survivor of a shipwreck that, as is seen later, epitomizes man's inhumanity to man, his greed, violence, envy, and treachery, all that is opposite to and a denial of love. In Arcadia, Musidorus's own experience of love will be enlarged and his initial response will need to be purged of grosser elements, but when he first arrives, his deepest experience of feeling for another has been for his friend, Pyrocles, and the shepherd friends recognize a kindred feeling that endears him to them.

Book 1 gives a great deal of attention to friendship and marks out the ground for much that is to follow. "True friendship," Kalander's steward tells Musidorus, "is so rare as it is to be doubted whether it be a thing in deed or but a word" (NA, 28; P, 87) Friendship, like love, can be professed without being meant and, like love also, can be vitiated by flaws of character. "None but such as are good men can give good things," Milton's Lady told Comus, and Sidney is equally clear that none but good men can be good friends. The virtues of Claius and Strephon are stressed, and the point is amplified later in the story of Tydeus and Telenor (NA, 184–87, 263–65; P, 280–83, 362–63). These two are most devoted and faithful friends of Plexirtus, but all the virtue of their selflessness and constancy is undermined by their wilful disregard of his great wickedness. They choose "rather to be good friends than good men," and they come to their deaths because of this. Pyrocles and Musidorus are not directly in danger of the same error, but the story of tainted friendship, like the story of Amphialus's tainted love, serves to emphasize the moral dangers and temptations lurking in the closest of personal relationships, and like Amphialus, Tydeus and Telenor fulfill the function of surrogates who channel off dangers that have the potential to destroy the princes.

What book 1 primarily shows, however, is that even the best-founded relationship is subject to strains and can only be sustained by the continued exercise of selflessness, and the willing surrender of self-will and self-interest to the welfare of the friend. Musidorus leads a force against the Helots in order to rescue Kalander's son, Clitophon, whom they have taken prisoner, and he engages in single combat with the Helots' captain. They are equally matched in skill and courage, and neither can gain advantage till the Helot captain strikes his adversary on the side of the head, causing his helmet to fall off. Instead of attacking the now unprotected head and face, the captain falls to his knees and offers to yield his sword. The Helot captain is, in fact, none other than Pyrocles, whose adventures, following the shipwreck that washed Musidorus ashore at the feet of Strephon and Claius, have brought him to this situation. Ariosto's Angelica and Spenser's Britomart also lose their helmets, and to great effect, but it is the identity, not the sex, of Musidorus that causes Pyrocles' surrender at a point when he might have triumphed. Sidney does not suggest that Pyrocles was tempted to any other course of action, but the episode gives early notice that between these two men, of whose accomplishments and qualities more is learned later, there is no question of rivalry, envy, or the wish to score off one another. On an earlier occasion, as the reader learns in book 2, Pyrocles had deliberately separated himself from Musidorus, wishing to undertake an adventure alone, but the reason for this was far from a desire to compete (NA, 235; P, 333). In their mature equality, each is both dependant and supporter and each gladly and freely takes every opportunity to praise the other and minimize his own achievement.

There is one other occasion in book 1 when Pyrocles and Musidorus come to blows. This is at the tournament that Basilius permits, at the request of Phalantus of Corinth, and in which a variety of participants compete to justify the claim that each one's mistress is the most beautiful. The tournament itself is thematically important in a number of ways but principally for its bearing on the theme of love and the potentially destructive collision between love and friendship.

Phalantus, the challenger, is carefully characterized by Sidney. He is a very attractive man, honorable and brave, a most agreeable companion and a faithful courtier in the service of Queen Helen whose bastard brother he is. He is, in fact, one of the hero figures, or potential hero figures, of *Arcadia,* Amphialus and Argalus being among them, against whom Pyrocles' and Musidorus's claims to heroic stature stand always to be judged. Phalantus, it transpires, with all his good qualities, is marred by a certain slackness. He is "not given greatly to struggle with his own disposition" (NA, 91; P, 154), and living for a time at the court of Laconia and being made much of there, he adopts the modish affectation of courtly love. As Basilius, speaking for once with an older man's wisdom, explains to Zelmane, this is love bred in idleness "for want of other business." "So therefore," Basilius continues, "taking love upon him like a fashion," Phalantus courted Artesia who, as shallow as he, treated him with haughty disdain. Sidney's description of their association amounts to a trenchant account of the charade of courtly love, and to be involved in it is a disgrace to both parties. Artesia is the more culpable in this instance because her behavior stems from serious moral misdirection (she has been brought up by Cecropia and proved a good disciple: this is among the signals in book 1 of Cecropia's later fully revealed villainy); but Phalantus's acceptance of folly leads him into an increasingly false position and finally to the point of issuing a challenge on behalf of a woman whom he has praised insincerely and to whom he has vowed a devotion he by no means feels. The end of this affair is as might be expected. Phalantus is unhorsed by an unknown knight in the last stages of the tournament, whereupon Artesia repudiates him. Phalantus, no longer obliged to pretend, responds that "the loss of such a mistress will prove a great gain" (NA, 104; P, 167). Basilius is amused at the ignominious collapse of this pretence love, which made such a show at the start and proved in the end so hollow.

Pyrocles and Musidorus have an active role in Phalantus's tournament. Pyrocles, already disguised as the Amazon Zelmane, disguises himself further in some uncouth armor that he borrows and, unrecognized, is encountered by Musidorus, himself in a black armor unfamiliar to Pyrocles. Each comes to challenge Phalantus in defense of his mistress's beauty, and neither knowing the other, they fall to fighting as to which should have the priority. Phalantus himself joins in, and the three-cornered fight is only ended by the personal intervention of Basilius. At the time of the tournament it is early in the princes' courtship, and their love has not been tested and strengthened by any trial of courage or endurance. They are, temporarily, like Phalantus, idle, having laid aside their princely roles, and their love may be tainted by the same self-indulgence and unreality as his. Pyrocles, who is accorded the privilege of fighting Phalantus first, defeats him and so makes the opening for the break-up of the spurious relationship with Artesia. The superiority of Pyrocles and the greater truthfulness of his feelings are thus established by comparison with Phalantus, though there is a long way for him and Musidorus to go before they may be able to stand comparison with Argalus.

In their encounter at the tournament, Pyrocles and Musidorus fight each other for precedence in a love contest. The friendship of Strephon and Claius was cemented by their mutual love for Urania, but Pyrocles and Musidorus and the young women they fall in love with are of commoner clay than the shepherds and their beloved. Their history is to be conducted on a more down-to-earth level and rivalry in love is potentially a dangerous threat. They fight with considerable bitterness at the tournament, and though all is well when they meet again, the issue of rivalry comes to the fore as soon as Musidorus begins to tell Pyrocles how he, formerly a disbeliever in love, has been incurably smitten. Sidney makes the most of the occasion. Pyrocles, hearing Musidorus declare himself in love, begins to fear that they are Philoclea's charms that have overcome him.

Musidorus, absorbed in his own story, keeps him in suspense, Pyrocles all the while "racked with jealousy" (NA, 107; P, 170–71). The ironic amusement with which Sidney treats this episode should not obscure its importance in the economy of the whole. It delights but it also instructs about what Sidney intends and especially what he does not intend to do with his principal characters and his themes of love and friendship. He knows as well as anyone that love and friendship can interfere with and even destroy each other. He knows also the view that male friendship is superior to the love of women. One way of resolving the tensions between friendship and love is that of Shakespeare's Valentine, when he makes over all his claims in Sylvia to Proteus, and there are plenty of variations on this idea;[6] but Sidney is not taking a high romantic line of that kind. "It is clear that Pyrocles and Musidorus, if they had fallen in love with the same princess, would have been deadly rivals":[7] perhaps so, but this is to speculate well out of the range of the text. Pyrocles and Musidorus are allowed one encounter as rival lovers at Phalantus's tournament. This stands as a token working off of any submerged animosity and jealousy, but after Musidorus's naming of Pamela as his beloved, the way is open for mutual support, encouragement, and assistance, in love as in all else, for the rest of the story. That love and friendship are not allowed to collide has many consequences of which the most important, ultimately, is that they do not have to be ranked in order of merit. Love of friend and love of woman are both worthy of the modern hero. Pyrocles and Musidorus do not have to choose between them, and they are the completer men for experiencing both.

The building up of the roles of Pamela and Philoclea in *New Arcadia* has an important bearing on the friends-lovers situation of the young men. The princesses themselves are "great friends" as well as sisters (NA, 276; P, 375), loyal and loving to each other (NA, 424–25; P, 556–57).[8] They are given not only beauty, to arouse desire, but also qualities of character that make them the equals of the men. There is no derogation in loving such as they are and friendship and love are seen as equally estimable values in the lives both of the young men and the young women.

The possibility that rivalry in love may impair the friendship of Pyrocles and Musidorus is glanced at in *Old Arcadia* (OA, 168–69) but comparison of the relevant passage with the scene between the two that has been described above illustrates again how matters that are lightly sketched in *Old Arcadia* are opened out to discover further perspectives in *New Arcadia*. The essentials are the same in both versions, including Pyrocles' feeling (of course) about the superior attractiveness of Philoclea, though this is, more delicately, kept to himself as a private opinion in the revised text; but the episode is at the same time made more amusing and charged with more implications in *New Arcadia*. As it stands there, it characterizes the dominant method of the new book 1, where ideas and attitudes that are to be decisive in the ethos of the whole work are subtly insinuated through narrative materials that have their own charm and provide varied entertainment.

A feature common to book 1 in both the original and the revised texts is the use of rhetorical speech in formal situations. Examples of public oratory designed to sway a mob are to be found in Pyrocles' address to the Helots (NA, 39, 40–41; P, 100, 101–2), though these are to be much surpassed by his performance in book 2 when Basilius's lodge comes under attack (NA, 283–87; OA, 129–31; P, 381–87); but the form of debate predominates and is in every respect of great importance.[9] All kinds of choices and judgments have to be made as events unroll, and now and then the process of enquiry and decision is formalized into a set-piece disputation in which evidence is analyzed and the pros and cons of specific issues are set out. The first example, in both texts, concerns Basilius's decision, because of the oracle's prediction, to retire to the forest and Philanax's advice to the contrary. The debate form is clearer in *Old Arcadia* where Basilius and Philanax deliver speeches to each other, one explaining the reasons for retirement, the other arguing cogently against them. The treatment is somewhat different in *New Arcadia* and Philanax delivers his arguments by letter, but none of the substance of the matter is lost as Philanax confutes Basilius's positions one by one. The second example, again in both texts, involves Pyrocles and Musidorus. Musidorus, like any well-trained young Renaissance gentleman, knows what to do when visiting a foreign country and, when he has done it, believes it is time to move on.[10] He is surprised that Pyrocles appears to be in no hurry. Accordingly, he launches upon a well-prepared and formal speech that opens with general moral propositions and proceeds to apply them to Pyrocles' reproach. Pyrocles counters with an interesting defense:

> "I find not myself wholly to be condemned because I do not with continual vehemency follow those knowledges which you call the bettering of my mind; for both the mind itself must, like other things, sometimes be unbent or else it will be either weakened or broken; and these knowledges, as they are of good use, so are they not all the mind may stretch itself unto. Who knows whether I feed not my mind with higher thoughts?" (NA, 50; OA, 14; P, 11)

This is a more daring rebellion against conventional wisdom than Musidorus is at this stage aware of, since the "higher thoughts" in fact are of Philoclea's perfections. As for his solitariness, Pyrocles says defiantly, "Eagles, we see, fly alone; and they are but sheep which always herd together." In solitude, he claims, he nurses his "higher" contemplations. He then veers off, apparently on a new tack, praising the natural beauties of Arcadia and concluding that it must be the habitation of a goddess. Herewith he looks mournfully at Musidorus who, for all his good will, is incapable of taking the broad hint. While Pyrocles spoke Musidorus had been busy rehearsing the main points of a proper debating answer to Pyrocles' defense of his solitariness but, fluent as he could be on that theme, he abandons it to follow instead the later line of Pyrocles' speech and to oppose a little skepticism to his friend's "excessive praises" of Arcadia. Perhaps, he suggests, Pyrocles has been occupying his solitary time in reading poets who "set up everything to the highest note; especially when they put such words in the mouths of one of these fantastical, mind-infected people that children and musicians call 'Lovers' " (NA, 52; OA, 17; P, 114). This brings Pyrocles to the brink of full confession, but the conversation is interrupted at that point in *New Arcadia* by the entry of Kalander inviting them both to go hunting. There is no interruption in *Old Arcadia*, which continues with a straightforward development of the situation.

The affinities with the style and substance of formal debates as practiced in schools and universities are clear in this scene, especially in the attitude of Musidorus. Other things are added, of course. Pyrocles' contributions have a subtext that Musidorus is trying to read, even while he practices his rhetorical skills. Pyrocles is torn between desire to conceal and desire to reveal what is ailing him, and Musidorus is partly sharp and partly obtuse. In the end Musidorus goes straight to the exposed nerve with his derogatory reference to lovers, but this seems to be accidental, for his reaction to Pyrocles' confession, when it comes, that he is such a "mind-infected" person, is one of shock and horror.

The next stage of development in the situation does not occur in *New Arcadia* till some time later when Musidorus comes upon an Amazon lady walking in a wood and recognizes that the "lady" is in fact his friend Pyrocles. The debate between them resumes at this point, sharper now because the situation has gone much further and the division in point of view is out in the open and seen to be radical. Musidorus begins with one of his well-composed speeches, adding point to point to build up a formidable attack on Pyrocles' position and finally expressing himself confident that his friend, convinced by his arguments, will be converted and abandon what is so unworthy of him and so damaging (NA, 70–72; OA, 18–20; P, 132–34).

The effect of his speech is not what he intended, for it rouses some anger in Pyrocles. He rejects Musidorus's contemptuous account of women and defends love itself rather in the same way that Sidney defends poetry against Plato's strictures in the *Apology for Poetry*. It is not love (or poetry) that is at fault but rather lovers (and poets) who are inadequate. Like Musidorus in their earlier exchange, he has much in mind that he might say to argue his points. " 'But these disputations,' he says, 'are fitter for quiet schools than my troubled brains, which are bent rather in deeds to perform than in words to defend the noble desire that possesseth me.' " There follows a rapid sequence of challenges by Musidorus and ripostes from Pyrocles, culminating like this:

> "Alas, let your own brain disenchant you," said Musidorus.
> "My heart is too far possessed," said Pyrocles.
> "But the head gives you direction," said Musidorus.
> "And the heart gives me life," answered Pyrocles.

Musidorus is grieved to see Pyrocles so bent, as he believes, on his own destruction and speaks, as Sidney puts it, "with more than accustomed vehemency." He is, in fact, very sharp indeed.

Clearly this verbal context is more dangerous to the friendship than either of the two physical combats discussed earlier. Two highly educated young men pit their wits against each other and fall naturally into reminiscence of the formal disputations with which they are familiar. Musidorus, in particular, is confident in the lessons that his training has taught him. Pyrocles is unyielding, but his arguments are more tentative. For Musidorus the definition of virtue is clear. It consists in the cultivation of the rational faculty and the maintenance of its clear preeminence over the senses and the passions. Pyrocles is feeling his way toward something else, which he cannot distinctly name. Musidorus speaks of the knowledge that may be gained from study and observation and experience, but Pyrocles has begun to think that this may not be all: "Truly, as I know not all the particularities, so yet I see the bounds of all these knowledges: but the workings of the mind I find much more infinite than can be led unto by the eye, or imagined by any that distract their thoughts without themselves" (NA, 50; OA, 14; P, 111).[11] Marlowe's Dr Faustus also saw the "bounds" of knowledge as the Middle Ages defined it, and sought to go beyond them by necromancy; but Pyrocles, a Renaissance man in spite of the ostensibly antique setting, is finding a new world to explore within his own personality. The sympathies and responses he finds there tell him that the traditional wisdom about women and love is untrue and that what the well-trained Musidorus thinks of as knowledge is severely limited. Yet what love is and what his new conception of virtue will demand he hardly knows as yet. Sexuality and sensuousness are obtrusive even as he speaks of loving virtue and of his wish "to prove himself a man." He does not so much answer Musidorus's charges as give earnest of his faith that they *can* be answered, and all he says and does gives testimony that the experience he is undergoing is not a trivial one. His reply to Musidorus's last speech—"Prince Musidorus," he calls him, a uniquely distancing form of address—is a reproach for his cruelty, after which he sinks to the ground, overcome with lovesickness on Philoclea's account and with the unkindness of his friend. Upon this, Musidorus abandons his critical rationalities and follows his heart, apologizing for his sharp speeches and vowing all help and comfort to Pyrocles in his love. The scene ends with humorous reversals, Musidorus chiding Pyrocles for being cruel to him and mocking his own previous confident righteousness.

These scenes between Pyrocles and Musidorus are evidently important in relation to the theme of friendship and even more important in relation to *Arcadia*'s explorations of the nature of love and the nature of virtue. Questions are raised here not by means of narrative episodes but in the academic form of debate, and it is noticeable that *New Arcadia* does not much change the *Old Arcadia* version, although it divides the original one scene into two parts. *Old Arcadia* concludes with an extended example of forensic debate in which the conduct of the princes and Gynecia is held up for close scrutiny and criticism, and they are pressed specifically about the quality of their love and how far they can justify their conduct as "virtuous." The form of the prophecy in *New Arcadia* makes it plain that the revised text was to move to a similar culminating point. In the new context, the rigorous final scrutiny of the princes' claims to love and virtue gains even sharper point, because of the wider scope and greater depth of inquiry into all issues that *New Arcadia* conducts. To the initiating and concluding debates, *New Arcadia* adds that in book 3 between Pamela and Cecropia, over the evidences for the existence of God, an addition that in itself indicates the depth of the foundations on which *New Arcadia* rests and the importance of debate as a characteristic feature of its structure.

There may be no better way of highlighting the quality of Sidney's work in book 1 than by comparison with Lyly's *Euphues*. Lyly might have been a man after Sidney's own heart. He was educated and clever, and he was devoting his talents to the refining and sophisticating of English writing. He was witty, he made his sentences pirouette and display, he dazzled and entertained with his parade of allusions, and, in *Euphues*, he applied all this brilliance to subjects that were worth writing about: virtue, love, friendship, education, women. In fact, Sidney seems to have been riled by Lyly. In *Astrophil and Stella* 3 he comments ironically on misguided handlers of fantasticated language:

> Let daintie wits crie on the Sisters nine,
> That bravely maskt, their fancies may be told:
> Or *Pindare*'s Apes, flaunt they in phrases fine,
> Enam'ling with pied flowers their thoughts of gold:
> Or else let them in statelier glorie shine,
> Ennobling new found Tropes with problems old:
> Or with strange similies enrich each line,
> Of herbes or beastes, which Ind or Afrike hold.

Clearly Lyly is one of the "daintie wits" aimed at, as he is in a well-known passage from *An Apology for Poetry:*

> Now for similitudes in certain printed discourse, I think all herbarists, all stories of beasts, fowls and fishes are rifled up, that they come in multitudes to wait upon any of our conceits; which certainly is as absurd a surfeit to the ears as is possible: for the force of a similitude not being to prove anything to a contrary disputer, but only to explain to a willing hearer; when that is done, the rest is a most tedious prattling, rather over-swaying the memory from the purpose whereto they were applied, than any whit informing the judgement, already either satisfied, or by similitudes not to be satisfied. [12]

Caring so deeply as he did about the enhancement of English literature and the language, Sidney was likely to be particularly exasperated that a gifted man like Lyly should set what seemed to him so spectacularly bad an example. Euphuism and Arcadianism, the styles of their respective books, have often been discussed as twin examples of affected writing, precious art styles equally aberrant from the true course of English writing, but it has at least to be acknowledged that both writers were addressing a real problem. Jonas Barish, in his "The Prose Style of John Lyly," reminds us that "for the first time, in the sixteenth century, native prose was shouldering the burden formerly carried by the learned languages. The excessive logicality of Lyly's style is merely one issue of a process that had been going on for decades; the search for a structural principle in English which would enable the language to deal adequately and in an ordered fashion with complex material, and thus do the work formerly done by the inflected endings of Latin."[13] R. W. Bond, the editor of Lyly, is in general unsympathetic to Sidney, but some of the praise he applies to Lyly has wider relevance: "the praise of asserting, with an emphasis hitherto unknown, the absolute importance to prose-writing of the principle of Design," "the quality of mind in style, the treatment of the sentence, not as a haphazard agglomeration of clauses, phrases and words, but as a piece of literary architecture."[14] When it came to solution of the problem, Sidney and Lyly parted company and Sidney's comment about the use of similes is essentially a criticism that Lyly's style is insufficiently intellectual. Eloquence and even logicality stop at the outside of words only: there is not sufficient mental pressure behind them to give real force and significance.

Sidney's work can, in fact, be read as almost a point-by-point correction of Lyly in both style and substance. *Euphues* moralizes sententiously, but Lyly's characters and their sentiments are superficial. Euphues and Philautus become bosom friends on short acquaintance, but Euphues betrays Philautus when he falls in love with Lucilla and the "friends" abuse each other. When Lucilla proves faithless to them both, they are reconciled and Euphues takes to writing long moral epistles to Philautus. Though friendship and love and the nature of virtue are main topics between them, there is nothing to compare either for liveliness or penetration with the debate that Musidorus and Pyrocles engage in, or with the investigations of the subjects that *New Arcadia* conducts through its multiple narratives. A telling comparison can be made between the *Arcadia* scenes in which Musidorus questions Pyrocles about his behavior and Pyrocles at last confesses his love, and an episode in *Euphues* (vol. 1, pp. 211–15). The situations are similar and many of the points made in the two scenes are the same, but *Euphues* quite lacks the dramatic qualities, the humor, and the humanity of *Arcadia*. In Lyly's episode Euphues deliberately deludes Philautus by pretending to be enamored of Livia, not Lucilla, and Lyly's comment is:

> Heere you may see gentlemen the falshood in felowship, the fraude in friendship, the painted sheth with the leaden dagger, ye faire woords that make fooles faine

—which speaks for itself about the nature of the friendship and about Lyly's method of dealing with his material.

Euphues and His England, a sequel that followed shortly after *Euphues*, has a dedication, "To the ladies and Gentlewomen of England," which contains the often-quoted sentence "Euphues had rather lye shut in a Ladyes casket, then open in a schollers studie" (2,

p. 9), but in fact the differences between *Euphues* and *Arcadia* are nowhere more striking than in the attitude their authors take toward women. Euphues, paying court to Lucilla, is extravagant in his praise of women: "I for mine owne part am brought into a Paradise by the onely imagination of woemens vertues, and were I perswaded that all the Divelles in hell were woemen, I would never live devoutly to inherite heaven, or that they were all Saintes in heaven, I woulde live more strictly for feare of hell" (2, p. 216). Euphues has no character and consequently no attributes, but Lyly himself is being witty here with an undercurrent of cynicism and it is no surprise to find such praise rapidly replaced by traditional opprobrium a few pages later as Euphues, rejected by Lucilla, laments his case:

> I had thought that women had bene as we men, that is true, faithfull, zealous, constant, but I perceive they be rather woe unto men, by their falshood, gelosie, inconstancie. (2, p. 241)

His "cooling card for Philautus and all fond lovers" squeezes every drop of enjoyment it can from the theme of the wickedness and worthlessness of women and then follows with a briefer address to "grave matrons and honest maidens," assuring them that the strictures do not, of course, apply to them. Lyly, in fact, is not serious except in his pleasure in seizing rhetorical opportunity.

The rhetoric thus becomes an end in itself and is, in quality and effect, quite different from Sidney's. A comparative analysis of Sidney's and Lyly's styles forms part of an article by P. Albert Duhamel, which concludes that "almost any page of *Arcadia* can be analysed to show Sidney's difference from his contempoaries . . . a careful and restrained use of ornament, and a subordination of that ornament to meaning."[15] The comparison with Lyly throws into very clear relief the extent to which Sidney's style, "artificial" as it is, is in its way functional, an instrument of meaning that is precise and finely tooled to make distinctions and establish ideas.[16] Lyly's, on the other hand, is sounding and ingenious, but as Prince Hal might put it, there is but one halfpenny worth of matter to an intolerable deal of art.

Sidney and Lyly were writing to and about Renaissance courtiers and the subjects that engaged their attention. Sidney works at a deeper level and with much more varied resources, and *Arcadia* retains a powerful capacity to teach and delight even in the twentieth century. It is a pity if a too narrow view of what constitutes good style acts as a deterrent and if unfamiliarity with rhetorical self-consciousness is allowed to obscure the fact that there are differences between the practitioners that go right to the heart of their works.

Sidney's style is the perfect medium for the intricately contrived, balanced, or antithetical narrative patterns of *Arcadia,* and to read with care is to find increasingly that not only is there no empty verbiage, but on the contrary, in passage after passage that may appear at first sight merely decorative, every word works.

(ii)

If book 1 of *New Arcadia* functions as an overture, sounding themes to be developed later, book 2 plunges its readers full into narrative complexity. Sidney's revised text is a remarkable tissue of dramatic action and narrative retrospection. Musidorus, Philoclea, Pamela, Pyrocles, and Basilius all in turn give extensive accounts of preceding events, and the cowardly traitor, Clinias, contributes an account of the background to the rebellion that takes place in the later chapters, Miso and Mopsa add to the quota of tales that are told in the book. Musidorus's stories, which fill in his and Pyrocles' past life for the information of Pamela, have a largely political emphasis, for they are concerned with the princes' encounters with a variety of rulers whose qualities are carefully discriminated by Musidorus. Philoclea, Pamela, and Basilius between them tell the story of Erona and Plangus, a long and complex history in itself. Pyrocles tells Philoclea of earlier adventures, as Musidorus has told Pamela, but his emphasis is on personal rather than public affairs, and women, and women's experience, are at the forefront of them. While the narratives are proceeding, Sidney does not allow the reader to forget the present scene. Musidorus, carried away by recollection of a moment of extreme stress, slips inadvertently from the third person to the first, and Pamela lets him know she has observed it: ". . . with that, Dorus blushed and Pamela smiled, and Dorus the more blushed at her smiling, and she the more smiled at his blushing, because he had, with the remembrance of that plight he was in, forgotten in speaking of himself to use the third person" (NA, 173; P, 268). Pyrocles excuses his account of Andromana's shameless wooing of himself and Musidorus: " 'Which proceeding of hers I do the more largely set before you, most dear lady, because by the foil thereof you may see the nobleness of my desire to you and the warrantableness of your favour to me' "; and Sidney records that: "At that Philoclea smiled with a little nod" (NA, 250; P, 348), thus, at one stroke, bringing the scene and the character alive. A little later Pyrocles is pulled up abruptly in his account of the shipwreck in which he and Musidorus were separated. " 'But what,' said Philoclea, 'became of your cousin, Musidorus?' 'Lost,' said Pyrocles," a monosyllabic answer that, from a young man as eloquent as he, amusingly indicates his embarrassment at this question. Philoclea follows up her advantage: " 'Ah, my Pyrocles,' said Philoclea, 'I am glad I have taken you. I perceive you lovers do not always say truly. As though I knew not your cousin Dorus the shepherd.' " Pyrocles comes out of it well: " 'Life of my desires,' said Pyrocles, 'what is mine, even to my soul, is yours, but the secret of my friend is not mine,' " and he adds, guessing where her information has come from, " 'But I perceive your noble sister and you are great friends, and well doth it become you so to be' " (NA, 276; P, 375). The punctuation of the narrative of past events by such small but telling intrusions of the present preserves the momentum of the main action and makes smooth transitions possible when the narrative voice changes from that of a character to that of the author himself, moving his plot forward to another phase of its development.

There is plenty of evidence that Sidney was perfectly well aware of the narrative character of book 2 and indeed that he was deliberately laying out and exploring narrative possibilities. In the language of contemporary criticism, book 2 consists largely of metanarrative. There is narrative, and there is narrative within narrative, and there are different approaches to narrative. Pyrocles/Zelmane reads Basilius's poetic record of the lamentations of Plangus and then comments to Philoclea, " 'Most excellent lady . . . one may be little the wiser for reading this dialogue since it neither sets forth what this Plangus is, nor what Erona is, nor what the cause should be which threatens her with death and him with sorrow' " (NA, 204; P, 301). The background of the story is then elicited, bit by bit, through contributions by various speakers distributed throughout book 2. The treatment of this story forms, in fact, a miniature reproduction of the method of the whole of books 1 and 2, which open with unexplained introductions and then proceed bit by bit to build up the history of preceding events, eventually arriving at the shipwreck whose aftermath is described, without explanation, in the first few pages of *New Arcadia*. The stories told by Miso and Mopsa, Dametas the Herdsman's wife and daughter, point particularly clearly to Sidney's interest in narrative method in book 2. Miso's story (NA, 210–12; P, 307–10) is a comic contrast to the chronicle of the loves and woes of high-born persons that it interrupts, and Sidney evidently delights in mingling kings and clowns in his fiction, however he disapproved of it in stage plays. But apart from the ironies and the parodic elements implicit in Miso's efforts, her story, with its crudities and its un-self-conscious salacity, has the robustness and temper of a medieval fabliau. In *Old Arcadia*, the poem abusing Cupid, which she has written in the back

of her prayer book, is spoken by Dicus in the First Eclogues (OA, 65–
66), where it merely makes one of a collection of views of love, but in
its setting in *New Arcadia* it gains greatly in point and comedy. The
poem itself is a piece of non-Petrarchan, anti-Cupid writing that Miso
takes literally and displays with pride. (It is of a kind, ostensibly
unsophisticated, that could only be composed by a sophisticated
writer.) It contributes to the effect of the whole episode in which the
earthy, uncourtly experience and attitudes of barber shops and village
streets and lecherous priests are both mocked by and mock the
courtly, storytelling gathering of princes and princesses. Miso's
"method" is rambling and naïve and, to tell it, she sat "on the ground
with her knees up, and her hands upon her knees, tuning her voice
with many a quavering cough." Mopsa's tale, like her mother's,
belongs to a pre-Renaissance world, but whereas Miso favors the
fabliau, Mopsa's taste, befitting her youth, is for romance (NA, 214;
P, 311–12). She "tumbles into" her story of a knight and a princess
and mysterious adventures involving a series of aunts and a trail of
nuts and scrambles together a remarkable assemblage of motifs from
folk narratives. *New Arcadia* itself is, like *Old Arcadia*, a romance, full
of knights and princesses and adventures (and including aunts) but
the significance of its episodes and the handling of its narrative are
worlds away from the simple-minded Mopsa's story of her anonymous
knight and her string of "And so . . . and so . . . and then. . . ."
Miso's story and Mopsa's are delightful in themselves, parodies of old
and unsophisticated narrative methods that are treated with affection
as well as with amusement. They not only add variety to the cento of
stories in book 2 and spice the affairs of the principals with a tang of
broader comedy, but they display also Sidney's active awareness, as
he was composing, of different ways in which story material can be
handled and his conscious development and manipulation of techniques and effects.

The same point can be illustrated in other ways. Musidorus speaks
for his creator when he lays down for Pyrocles in book 1 a narrative
prescription: "'I pray you again tell me,' he says, 'but tell it me fully,
omitting no circumstance, the story of your affections, both beginning
and proceeding. . . . Let me receive a clear understanding, which
many times we miss while those things we account small, as a speech
or a look, are omitted, like as a whole sentence may fail of his
congruity by wanting one particle'" (NA, 78; P, 140).[17] The importance of detail that reveals, animates, authenticates, is manifest in all
sorts of situations in *New Arcadia*. The details themselves may stem
from sympathetic observation of the natural world or amused
awareness of the ways of human beings, as in these two examples

from the same scene in book 2: the heron seen "getting up on his waggling wings with pain till he was come to some height (as though the air next to the earth were not fit for his great body to fly through)"; and Dametas driving home "half sleeping, half musing about the mending of a vine-press" (NA, 142–43; P, 236). Most often detail is used to give a dramatic immediacy, and Sidney's interest in dramatic effect is strikingly evident. He frequently sees his characters as though they are acting on a stage in front of him, and he writes what might well be stage directions. By details of gesture and expression he strives to make narrative embody the living moment, "to make you hear, to make you see," as another storyteller puts it. He tries similarly to indicate how a speech should be spoken so as to convey more than the surface meaning of the words. In the following examples, the device is the same, merely the use of parenthesis, but the effects achieved are quite different. The first is Pyrocles telling Philoclea of the original Zelmane's unhappy love for him: " 'Such was therein my ill destiny, that this young lady Zelmane (like some unwisely liberal, that more delight to give presents than to pay debts) she chose (alas for the pity) rather to bestow her love (so much undeserved as not desired) upon me than to recompense him whose love (besides many other things) might seem (even in the court of honour) justly to claim it of her. But so it was (alas that so it was) whereby it came to pass that (as nothing doth more naturally follow his cause than care to preserve and benefit doth follow unfeigned affection) she felt with me what I felt of my captivity . . .' " (NA, 252; P, 350–51). If embarrassment at telling this tale of devoted but unrequited love to the girl he wants to marry makes part of Pyrocles' emotion here, it is only a small part. The qualifications and interjections speak rather of emotional involvement in a story often dwelt upon in recollection and pressing upon Pyrocles again as he retells it, with all its pathos and misfortune for both Zelmane and Palladius, her unfavored suitor. Palladius's story moves Pyrocles so much that when he comes to his death "the tears stand in his eyes" (NA, 258; P, 357), and, as for Zelmane, it is her name he adopts when he assumes his Amazon disguise.

The second example is from the speech of Clinias, the traitor, to Basilius, answering his request for an account of the origins of the rebellion by country people that has just been put down. The speech is a long one and it ends like this: ". . . they who first pretended to preserve you, then to reform you (I speak it in my conscience and with a bleeding heart) now thought no safety for them without murdering you. So as if the gods (who preserve you for the preservation of Arcadia) had not showed their miraculous power, and that they had not used for instruments both your own valour (not fit to be spoken of by so mean a mouth as mine) and some, I must confess, honest minds (whom, alas, why should I mention, since what we did reached not to the hundredth part of our duty?) our hands (I tremble to think of it) had destroyed all that for which we have cause to rejoice that we are Arcadians" (NA, 293; P, 392). The parentheses here are the carriers of Clinias's unctuousness and his flattery of Basilius and indicate quite plainly the tone of voice and the manner in which the words are delivered.

Clinias, a new character in the revised text with no counterpart in *Old Arcadia*, is altogether an interesting figure. His first introduction produces a little dramatic shock, since it is quite unprepared for and unexpected. Pyrocles has successfully played his last card in persuading the rebels to disperse peaceably when another voice is suddenly heard: "O weak trust of the many-headed multitude whom inconstancy only doth guide to well-doing!" (NA, 288; OA, 131; P, 387).[18] The unexpected comment raises an immediate question about the identity of the speaker. It is Clinias, "a crafty fellow," one who "in his youth had been a scholar so far as to learn rather words than manners, and of words rather plenty than order; and oft had used to be an actor in tragedies, where he had learned (besides a slidingness of language) acquaintance with many passions and to frame his face to bear the figure of them: long used to the eyes and ears of men, and to reckon no fault but shamefastness. . . ." He has, in fact, been a principal stirrer-up of the trouble, for he is an instrument of Cecropia, but for Basilius's hearing he plays the role of loyal citizen. The language applied to him is markedly theatrical. Addressing the mob "as if he had had a prologue to utter, he began with a nice gravity to demand audience. But few attending what he said, with vehement gesture as if he would tear the stars from the skies, he fell to crying out. . . ." When asked by Basilius for an account of the origin of the uprising, he first dips his hand in the blood of a wound he has suffered: "Then stretching out his hand, and making vehement countenances the ushers to his speeches, in such manner of terms recounted this accident."[19] Clinias's grandiloquent style and posturing contrast comically with his real ignominy. His cunning is dangerous, nonetheless, and certainly too much for Basilius, who "was not the sharpest piercer into masked minds" and who "took a good liking to him" (NA, 293; P, 392).

Clinias's role will be extended in further unsavory ways in book 3, but his appearance as actor in book 2 is particularly interesting for the way in which it points to a peculiar characteristic of the narrative in *New Arcadia*. This is not confined to book 2, but given the multiplicity of narrative voices there, it is pertinent to discuss it at this point. Sidney adopts from Heliodorus a method of interlocking narratives.[20] The effect, however, is quite different from that of his model. On the one hand, the interlacing of threads, the anticipations and echoes, engender a sense of security: the author has everything under a firm control that looks easy though it cannot really be so; his accomplishment in coordinating the disparate material and managing the ramifications of the narrative is an impressive example of the *sprezzatura*— easy mastery—that Castiglione commended. But there is another and paradoxically different effect of Sidney's narrative method. A great deal of the storytelling is delegated to the principals themselves, but other characters, both major and minor, are also called upon to relate past history. This is a particularly prominent feature of book 2, but it has also occurred in book 1. There, for example, Kalander gives Musidorus an account of the recent history of Arcadia, making use in the course of his recital of a letter written by Philanax to Basilius and picked up and copied by Clitophon, Kalander's son. The line by which information is transmitted is devious, but in this instance, it is at least reliable. In the Arcadian world this is by no means always so. A good deal of false information is disseminated at various times, not only by disreputable characters but by the princes themselves. Musidorus, for example, gives Menalcas a quite false account of his background and his intentions, deceiving the trusting shepherd by this invention (NA, 108; P, 172), and Pyrocles misrepresents himself to Basilius and his family when he pretends to be niece to the queen of the Amazons. Two other episodes, occurring in *Old Arcadia*, which Sidney might or might not have retained, at least indicate how the idea of deception in various forms was an integral part of *Arcadia* from its inception. The first is the fictitious account of his prehistory, one made deliberately dishonorable to himself, which Pyrocles gives to Gynecia in the cave (OA, 204; P, 656). The second is of a subtler kind. Gynecia delivers a just and noble reproof to Basilius for his dereliction of duty as husband, father, and king (OA, 277; P, 727)— only Gynecia, who had hoped to take her pleasure of Pyrocles, is not a qualified person to give it. Though what she says is valid, the speech is deceitful.

Lies and deceptions make up a great deal of Helidorus's narrative tissue. S. L. Wolff remarks on the prevalence of lying in these stories and points out that the lies are often perfectly gratuitous, not serving any purpose but simply born of the love of lying. To put this another way, the authors as fiction makers delight in their power to invent and fantasticate with gay abandon to show that they are not exhausted. Sidney too seems to have enjoyed inventing and may well have shared this impulse. If so, he made use of it in sophisticated ways and turned it to purposes of his own. Lies and deceptions carry multiple significances in *New Arcadia*.

They belong, at one level, to the metafictional quality of the work. The exuberance with which alternative narratives are invented and often invested with detailed plausibility draws attention to the fictitious nature of the whole book. After all, any of the "false" stories could equally well be as "true" as those which the main structure endorses. It is *all* a fiction, and one story has no more status than another, save by arbitrary decision. The alternative narratives stimulate readers' minds to travel a little way down the paths they offer, and the sense of the width of possibility in human experience is quickened. Beyond the area where attention is focused in *New Arcadia*, there lie further and further regions reaching toward unknown boundaries. Just as situations contain multiple possibilities, so also do characters. Pyrocles may become a woman and share, in some measure, women's experience. Musidorus may become a shepherd and put himself under Dametas's instruction. Each of them goes under several names at various stages of the narrative and in some ways seems to merge another life with his own, as Pyrocles takes the name of the dead Zelmane and Musidorus that of her lover Palladius. Personality, like event, has many dimensions and is capable of taking many shapes—this is a perception that the Elizabethan and Jacobean drama that Sidney never saw would make much of, as play after play sets in action characters who explore possibilities outside their normal range.[21]

To say that the heroes are role-playing is to be consistent with the dramatic interest Sidney displays throughout. He would have found frequent theatrical references in Heliodorus and Achilles Tatius, and when he wrote *Old Arcadia* he responded to dramatic example by dividing it into five acts.[22] Yet as the figure of Clinias bears witness, he was also distrustful of what the theater might stand for, and here some distinctions are called for. Though Pyrocles and Musidorus play parts that are not their own, they are not called upon in doing so to do much *acting*. Pyrocles' disguise as the Amazon warrior licenses him to be martial and to take initiatives, and it requires little simulation. Musidorus accepts the humility of his position with Dametas but scarcely makes a good show of shepherdly skills. Sidney draws attention to his incompetence in an amusing scene in which Dametas is for once clearly the superior (NA, 126; P, 220). The "performances" of Pyrocles and Musidorus in their adopted roles are very different in scope and character from those of Clinias and different again from those of Plexirtus, unrelievedly villainous father of the virtuous

Zelmane. Clinias has been a professional actor and every inch of him is a sham. Plexirtus has a different background, but intense wickedness teaches him both to simulate and dissimulate very convincingly. There is, in fact, a sharp moral difference between the "deceptions" practiced by the princes in their disguises and the "acting" of Clinias and Plexirtus: for the princes their role-playing becomes a means of extending and deepening their personalities and chastening their egos; for Clinias and Plexirtus it is a confirming and enforcing of already evil natures. Their "masked minds" are at all times a great threat to all with whom they are in contact.

This leads to another aspect of the nature of deception as Sidney employs it in the narrative economy of *New Arcadia*, for however enriching its possibilities as a narrative technique, Sidney is not the man to ignore its moral implications. The use of deception as a major narrative device has multiple effects, some specific, some pervasive. With so much tale-telling going on, auditors within the book and readers who peruse it are jointly involved in a process of assessment. Characters and readers alike need to take account of who is speaking as a tale is told and identify, if possible, the motives that are shaping or creating it. The reader has the advantage over the characters here and soon comes to realize that few things are fixed and definite. Appearances may cover several layers of deception: men and women may deceive themselves (as Amphialus does); others may speak truly even when they mean to deceive (as in Gynecia's speech to Basilius); some may be deceived because in the simplicity of their hearts they look for no deception (such as Leucippe, who is to be a victim of Pamphilus); some deceptions are knowingly wicked, others appear to be justified. "Craft against vice we must employ," as Shakespeare's Duke puts it in *Measure for Measure,* and Pyrocles and Musidorus before him have no scruple about the use of craft to serve their ends.

Misinformation, disguise, and deception and the mediating of narrative through other voices than that of an omniscient narrator produce up to a point a misty world: "in such a shadow or rather pit of darkness the wormish mankind lives" (OA, 385; P, 817), as Sidney comments when the last but one of the most sensational confusions occurs and Euarchus and the princes fail to recognize each other as father and son, uncle and nephew. The last of all concerns Basilius and the deceptive appearance of death in "a living man."

When truth is so hard to perceive, and when to act with straightforward and open honesty would be to ensure frustration and possibly danger, the difficulties of maintaining an honorable course are evidently very great. The most poignant and penetrating comment on the devious deceptions into which the princes have been led comes from Philoclea when Pyrocles attempts to explain the reasons for his apparent neglect and urges her to flee with him (OA, 234–35; P, 686). By a scale of absolute values, perhaps he deserves her cutting reproach, but in the world that Sidney depicts, Pyrocles' conduct is forgivable. It is a world where even paragons of virtue may be tainted and men genuinely struggling to keep faith with their own high ideals may against their wills be led into error. Their actions and motives are, in any case, liable to misinterpretation. Human judgment, trying to make distinctions and award sentence, is in the circumstances itself likely to be a prey to delusion, as Philoclea has misunderstood Pyrocles' actions, and as Euarchus is later to discover. Contradictions grow "in those minds which neither absolutely climb the rock of virtue nor freely sink into the sea of vanity" (NA, 232; P, 329),[23] and even the chaste and innocent Philoclea is not free of them. Sidney asks for charity in judgment, for the path of virtue is not only difficult to follow but difficult even to discern.

The fluctuating outlines, the confusions of good and evil, the simulation and dissimulation that are characteristic of the narrative methods as a whole reflect the similar shadings in the treatment of the characters that have already been described. In the assessment of characters and following of the narrative complexity Sidney is asking for active participation on the part of his readers, who must match scene to scene and lay one strand of action and comment against another to obtain a full view of Amphialus, say, or of Pamela. It is necessary to observe, weigh, and discriminate in order to assess. And as the characters talk, as they tell their stories, true and false, drawn from an apparently inexhaustible source, it is again required to consider, remember, fit piece to piece, and, noting who speaks and why, allow this knowledge to influence the understanding of what is spoken. For the reader all this is possible because the evidence is there, devised and carefully distributed by the author. Though for the characters the outlines of truth may be confused and blurred, the author exercises an understanding beyond their reach. Illusion and uncertainty are thus contained within security. Judgments of men may err, but providence will ensure that there is no ultimate or irremediable misunderstanding. The author, of course, *is* providence, for this is his created world, one of threat and error, but not without a plan. It is the peculiar quality of *New Arcadia* that its narrative methods both enact confusion and guarantee security.[24] When Webster, some thirty years later, wrote *The Duchess of Malfi* he remembered, or half-remembered, Sidney's comment: " 'Oh, this gloomy World,' " Bosola exclaims, having been instrumental in murdering the Duchess and, trying to save Antonio, having killed him too, "by mistake":

> Oh, this gloomy world!
> In what a shadowy, or deep pit of darkness
> Doth womanish[25] and fearful mankind live!

Webster borrows Sidney's words (nearly), but his two great plays *The White Devil* and *The Duchess of Malfi* are quite different in conception and worldview from Sidney's *Arcadia*. The mist does not clear from Webster's drama, though minor characters pronounce conventional moral wisdom at the end of the plays and the Duchess kneels to enter heaven, but the sun shines at the end of *Arcadia*, as love and forgiveness predominate and new life is promised for the princes and princesses in the "admirable fortunes" of their children.

New Arcadia shows Sidney keenly engaged in analyzing and deploying narrative methods, and the story of Plangus and Erona, as it stands in *Old Arcadia* and as it is developed in *New*, mainly in book 2, is a major exemplification of this. The comparison of the texts is worth making both because of the kind of expansion that takes place in the revised version and because of the placing of the narrative and the treatment of it.

In *Old Arcadia* the story is told by a young shepherd called Histor as a warning to his hearers to pay due respect to Cupid. It concerns Erona, daughter of the king of Lycia, who was offended by the many pictures and images of the naked god and had them all either defaced or pulled down. Cupid soon takes his revenge. Within twelve months Erona falls most unsuitably in love with a young man called Antiphilus, the son of her nurse, and for his sake refuses marriage with the great king of Persia. Her father brings all kinds of pressure to bear upon her, but she resists all that he can do and eventually her father dies of a broken heart. Parthenia, it is remembered, similarly resisted all the pressure that a mother and an unwelcome suitor could bring upon her to desert Argalus—but Argalus was worthy of her courage and devotion and Antiphilus is not: the two cases, so similar and yet fundamentally dissimilar, provide another example of Sidney's repeated insistence that a virtue is a virtue only if all the conditions are right.

Her father having died and Erona become queen, she intends to marry Antiphilus, but before she can do so, the rejected king of Persia makes war on her in an attempt to make her accept his suit instead. Antiphilus is captured and the king bargains his life for Erona's consent to marriage with him. Pyrocles and Musidorus, who have come to Erona's assistance, free Antiphilus and kill the king, thereby incurring the bitter animosity of the king's sister, Artaxia, who by her brother's death becomes queen of Persia. Erona marries Antiphilus, and Pyrocles and Musidorus depart from Lycia. Cupid then pursues his revenge further, for Antiphilus has become enamored of Artaxia during the time of his captivity and he now nurses ambitions of becoming king of Persia. He sends a secret message to her that he will do away with Erona if she will consent to become his wife. Artaxia, a shrewd and ruthless woman, uses his folly to trap both Antiphilus and Erona. She has him killed and Erona imprisoned. At the end of two years Erona will be publicly burned at the stake unless Pyrocles and Musidorus come to do battle on her behalf against superior odds. Artaxia believes that they will accept this challenge and will be killed, whereupon Erona will burn and her own revenge for her brother's death will be fully accomplished. Plangus, an Iberian nobleman who has fallen in love with Erona in her imprisonment, offers to find Pyrocles and Musidorus and tell them of Erona's need, but after a whole year of searching, he has failed to find them. He has arrived in Arcadia and has been overheard making "most wailful lamentation" (OA, 67).

The story recurs in *New Arcadia* but is told differently. It now begins *in medias res* with the lament of a stranger (Plangus) whose grief so impresses Basilius when he encounters him that he writes down the words in which he has expressed his sorrows. In *Old Arcadia* Plangus's lament is given at a point after Histor has told his story (OA, 147–52), but in *New Arcadia* its placing leads Pyrocles to remark that presenting the lament before giving the background leaves the reader in the dark. His comment (quoted previously in this chapter) is distinctly a literary critical one for, in fact, Pyrocles does know who Erona and Plangus are, having been personally involved in the early stages of the story—Musidorus has already referred to it in talking to Pamela (NA, 137; P, 231). Pyrocles is, in effect, reflecting the position of a reader of *New Arcadia* coming afresh to its opening pages and confronted without explanation with situations whose extensive pre-history is necessary information but is deferred until later. Pyrocles as reader draws attention to the method and also testifies to its effectiveness because he at once asks to be enlightened about the whole story. Sidney himself is, so to speak, an amused and interested overhearer of Pyrocles' remarks.[26] When he wrote *Old Arcadia* he knew his audience of "fair ladies" and addressed them frequently. He could gauge his success in entertaining them and engaging them in his story by actually seeing and hearing how they received it. When he wrote *New Arcadia* the situation changed. What he wrote then was to be read by unknown readers in unknown circumstances, and it is evident that he thought a good deal about ways of stimulating response and participation. Pyrocles' comment on Plangus's lament makes explicit one interest of the critical intelligence at work throughout in the construction and handling of the fiction.

At Pyrocles' request Philoclea begins to tell the tale of Erona, from her first contempt for Cupid till her marriage to Antiphilus. Her account follows the main lines of that given by Histor in *Old Arcadia* though there are a number of verbal changes. Among them it is worth noticing that when the rejected suitor (named as Tiridates, king of Armenia, in this version) makes war on Erona, in *Old Arcadia* he threatens that he will "have her either by force or otherwise," but in *New Arcadia* he vows instead "to win her or lose his life" (NA, 206; P, 303). At other points in *New Arcadia* Sidney shows himself more sensitive about suggestions of sexual violence than he had been in *Old Arcadia*. Here he removes a hint of it even in a general context of violence.

Pyrocles and Musidorus come to the rescue of Erona as they do in *Old Arcadia*, but at this point a considerable expansion of the original begins to take place. In the earlier version, only one sentence is needed for the princes to enter the city and bring the king to offer to settle the issue by single combat, but in *New Arcadia* the actions and motives of both sides are given in some detail, as is Erona's internal debate when she is faced with the choice between marrying Tiridates and condemning Antiphilus to death. One consideration after another prevails with her, and even after she has at length sent a message of surrender, she changes her mind and calls on Pyrocles and Musidorus to try by force of arms to rescue Antiphilus and so free her from the horns of her dilemma. They do so, killing Tiridates in the process, and Antiphilus and Erona are married. As in the earlier version, Antiphilus, once married, grossly fails to appreciate his debt to Erona and has the folly to think that he may be acceptable to Artaxia. He does not, in the revised text, contemplate murdering Erona to make a second marriage possible but, more characteristically, passes an "unlawful law" (NA, 299; P, 399) allowing more than one wife. Artaxia encourages him for her own ends, and he presses his suit all the more urgently when, to his pique, he finds himself cold-shouldered by other princes from whom, in his vanity, he expected deference. As before, he is tempted into a trap, and both he and Erona are put in irons, Artaxia planning to sacrifice them both on her brother's tomb.

What happens after the marriage is given succinctly in *Old Arcadia*, but again there is a major expansion in *New Arcadia*. Sidney builds the story out so that it becomes a tale of intermingled personal and political actions and motives, a fusion of private and public morals such as is characteristic of the treatment of governors and government in the revised text. Earlier in book 2 Musidorus, recounting to Pamela his adventures before coming to Arcadia, tells of encounters with a variety of tyrants and describes carefully the psychological make-up that in each case leads to their behavior and inflicts sufferings upon their people. Antiphilus now joins his gallery as the weak man who abuses power not because he positively ill-treats his subjects but because he is incapable of rising to the demands of his high position and demeans both himself and it. Suddenly raised to authority, he imagines there "was no so true property of sovereignty as to do what he listed and to list whatsoever pleased his fancy," and "he quickly made his kingdom a tennis-court where his subjects should be the balls" (NA, 299; P, 398). Vain and foolish, he falls prey to flatterers, who mislead him as a king, and by their sycophancy undermine him also as a man. Antiphilus, of course, is of lowly birth and not trained to kingship; he contrasts very strongly in that as in other respects with Pyrocles and Musidorus, whose exemplary upbringing is described earlier, the point being made "that a habit of commanding was naturalized in them, and therefore the further from tyranny" (NA, 164; P, 259).[27] But the significance of Antiphilus's misdemeanors is at least as much moral as social: there is, after all, no dearth of bad rulers of unimpeachable descent among the examples Sidney offers for study. Antiphilus is a mean figure in every way, and nurture and nature reflect upon each other. As a man and as a political figure he is a disaster, moral failure being inextricably entwined with political failure. This is a point that Sidney repeatedly makes, most strikingly in the story of the Paphlagonian king (NA, 179–85; P, 275–81).[28]

In *New Arcadia* Antiphilus's humiliations continue yet further than in the older text, for Plangus, moved with love of Erona and willing to save Antiphilus for her sake, plans to rescue him from his prison. Antiphilus, however, nearly causes the death of Plangus by his cowardly stupidity and he guarantees his own. He dies hated and held in contempt, at the hands of women who are his mortal enemies because of his law licensing polygamy. His "false-hearted life" is a pattern of public and private baseness.

As for Erona, her conduct in choosing wrongly in love has led her to loss and grief. Her people have turned against her, and like Antiphilus, she suffers deep personal humiliation because of her faults. She had once been self-willed and stubborn, but now she abases herself on behalf of a man whom everyone despises and who despises her. When he seeks Artaxia in a second marriage, "beyond all other examples of ill-set affection, she was brought to write to Artaxia that she was content, for the public good, to be a second wife and yield the first place to her; nay to extol him, and even woo Artaxia for him" (NA, 300; P, 400). "For the public good" is an ironic touch, as the women make clear when they force Antiphilus to pay dear for his lawmaking. Erona's letter to Artaxia is a prime example of public and private folly. Sidney's attitude toward her is nevertheless quite different from that he adopts toward Antiphilus. Erona has erred greatly, but the self-sacrificing love she shows her wretched husband earns Sidney's pity and even respect. Her sufferings are just punishment for her mistakings, as the miserable end of Tydeus and Telenor, men who devote priceless friendship to a worthless object, is of theirs, but Sidney triumphs over neither Tydeus and Telenor nor over Erona. Her story, in particular, is offered rather as an example of how even the good may be defeated by the twin difficulty of controlling their own natures and recognizing the true nature of others. A woman as capable of nobility as Erona may go astray, especially in the grip of the powerful emotion of love. The charity and sympathy Sidney extends to Erona is another example of the compassion he shows throughout *New Arcadia* to those who struggle, sometimes successfully, sometimes not, to walk the narrow way of the good life. It seems likely that, in the unwritten part of the revised *Arcadia*, Plangus, assisted by the princes, would have been allowed to rescue Erona and that they would find happiness together, having learned through prolonged and painful experience how truly to respect love by devoting it to a proper and worthy object. Cupid's revenge, which Histor is so concerned about in *Old Arcadia*, acquires, like many other episodes of the earlier text, a fuller significance in the *New*.

The treatment of Plangus himself is in *New Arcadia*, an important element in this significance. In *Old Arcadia* his part does not go much beyond his quest for the princes and his lament over Erona's sufferings and his own powerlessness to relieve her. In *New Arcadia* it goes a great deal further, and the narrative is taken back to a time years before, when Plangus was growing up in the court of his father, the king of Iberia. While he was still very young, Plangus entered into a liaison with a married woman. When his father discovered this, Plangus, protecting the woman's reputation at the expense of his own, vowed that, though he had been guilty of trying to seduce her, her chastity had been indefeasible. His father is only too well persuaded by these protestations and becomes infatuated with the woman himself. He sends Plangus, whom he now sees as a rival, out of the country, and when the husband dies, he marries the widow. She for her part is by no means passive in this train of events, for she plays the old king like a fish, till she has him safely hooked in marriage; she is, in fact, one of *Arcadia*'s skillful actors, her deceitful performance reaching a high level of accomplishment. When Plangus returns after some years of absence, he finds the king married and with a new son and daughter. Andromana, now his step-mother, tempts him again to become her lover but he refuses her advances bitterly. She determines to ruin him, before he can ruin her, by revealing their past relationship. She proceeds to poison his father's mind against him and to insinuate that Plangus is plotting to usurp the throne.[29] Finally she devises and enacts a little theatrical scene so contrived as to appear to prove incontovertibly that Plangus intends to murder his father.[30] Plangus is forced to flee the country and takes refuge at the court of Tiridates who becomes Erona's unwelcome suitor. There he encounters Erona and Antiphilus when they are captured.

The prehistory of Plangus as recounted by Pamela in book 2 of *New Arcadia* thickens the weave of personal and political strands in this pattern of stories. Plangus abuses love by his casual dalliance with another man's wife.[31] Then by his false gallantry in lying on her behalf he entraps his father and subjects him to an evil influence. The state is disturbed by rumors and suspicions, and the king might even have been deposed by an armed insurrection had not Plangus restrained the supporters who rise on his behalf. The king himself, of course, is far from blameless, since in his old age he allows himself, even before her husband's death, to lust for the woman. Afterward he lets her lead him by the nose and deteriorates so far as to employ a servant to poison his son. Plangus and Erona thus have both loved unworthily and have sins against love to expiate. If they are to come to a happy ending it must be through penitence and penance. Their stories in the revised book 2 form an important part of the web of narrative concerned with moral choices, and like the other stories, they carry implications that ramify extensively and link up with other episodes and divers themes. How deliberate this is can be observed by noticing that the material relating to Plangus is not entirely new. His relations with Andromana and what came of them have parallels in a similar story in *Old Arcadia* that occurs soon after Histor's recital of Plangus's lament (OA, 156–58). It concerns again a stepmother and her wanton passion for her stepson, and it is told in *Old Arcadia* as part of a recital by Histor of the many adventures and good deeds of Pyrocles and Musidorus before they came to Arcadia. It has no direct relation to Plangus, but in revision Sidney picked it up and refashioned it, dovetailing it into the story of Plangus and Erona and making it, not a discrete episode, but part of a continuous chronicle bearing significance at all points. Its combination of political and personal interests spans and links together the major emphasis of Musidorus's stories with their tales of tyrants and other governors and that of Pyrocles' stories, which are largely concerned with relationships on a more personal level.

The story of Plangus and Erona, told in a linearly straightforward way in *Old Arcadia*, is given extraordinarily complicated treatment in *New Arcadia*, and in its gathering of major themes and its technical virtuosity it stands as an epitome of the whole text, inset within the larger framework. The ingenuity of its manipulation and its virtuoso quality are highlighted—deliberately no doubt—by the mock narratives of Miso and Mopsa that interrupt it. That *New Arcadia* should have built into it a critique of narrative and a demonstration of kinds of storytelling, varying from the utterly artless to the most artfully contrived, is not at all surprising. Sidney, after all, was the writer of the first English critical essay, and when he wrote his sonnet sequence, *Astrophil and Stella*, he included in it many poems on how to write love poems. He was a highly self-conscious writer who knew very well what he was doing and found, or invented, many different things to do. The story of Plangus and Erona, beginning in the middle, returning to different points in the past, gradually filling in the whole picture, and mediating the various stages of the story through a number of tellers, duplicates the methods of *New Arcadia* as a whole—as no doubt Sidney very well knew and intended. The story is part of the self-reflexive system of *New Arcadia* and part of a "game" Sidney is playing with his verbal constructs; but for Sidney words can be made to work not merely within a linguistic frame but also to bear upon experience. The story of Plangus and Erona, again like *New Arcadia* as a whole and the other individual stories within it, makes a firm claim to cast a light on experience outside the world of the book. He wrote with the greatest commitment to the art of writing, devoting all his intelligence to it and evidently enjoying immensely the exercise and development of his powers, but the truth is, as Fulke Greville put it: "his end was not writing, even while he wrote": he looked beyond the page to "life and action."[32] Fiction was reality better understood: that was its justification and the justification also of the time, the intellectual labor, and the love he was prepared to give it and did so lavishly give.

(iii)

Book 1 of *New Arcadia* anticipates themes and events that are to be further treated later, and book 2 consists largely of retrospective narratives telling of events that occurred before the story opened. By means of these narratives, themes that were first sounded in book 1 are more fully developed, notably love and friendship, and some that were less firmly indicated earlier come into prominence—questions of government and the moral dilemmas created by an uncertain world of shifting and maybe delusory appearances. In book 2 also, Sidney's interest in the art of writing itself emerges clearly and is emphasized by the variety of narrative methods employed. Book 2 thus develops out of book 1, widening the field all the time, and both of them develop out of *Old Arcadia*, extending and rearranging old material but still allowing comparisons to be made. Book 3, to the contrary, deals with events that are entirely new to the revised text as the anticipations of book 1 and the retrospection of book 2 converge in a violent present, and issues that have been raised more or less explicitly earlier are heightened and developed to crisis point. This last point is most obviously true of the political element, with the kidnapping of the princesses and Amphialus's defiance of the king.

Basilius, both as man and ruler, has many weaknesses, and personal and public failings combine to open the peaceable and prosperous state he inherited to unrest and rebellion. At the same time, his sister-in-law, Cecropia, is working for her own ends to subvert his rule, and the two kinds of threat to good government and stability come into dangerous conjunction in book 3. When Amphialus fails to repudiate his mother's abduction of the princesses and sets himself to make what profit he can from it, his rank, reputation, courage, and intelligence put the lawful authority vested in Basilius in very great danger indeed. Amphialus is not only a brave and skillful soldier and an effective leader of men, but, guided by his mother, he shows himself to be also a clever politician. Having decided on rebellion, he first seeks allies and goes on to make a public justification of his actions, representing himself as the guardian, not the attacker, of the state, activated by public duty to save Basilius from unwise courses and by a sense of his own particular responsibilities as, he reminds Arcadians, the next male heir. By a mixture of well- and ill-grounded accusations and claims to be acting disinterestedly, together with hints that to match one of the princesses with himself would be a suitable resolution of the whole situation, Amphialus succeeds in persuading some to join him and in discouraging others from taking arms against him. Amphialus's rebellion reproduces in a higher key that of the common people earlier, and Cecropia is a dominant influence on both. Through Clinias, she stirred up the plebians to complain of Basilius's conduct and exploited their weaknesses to make them vulnerable to suggestion; similarly, she uses Amphialus's love for Philoclea to make him malleable to her purpose and stands at his shoulder as he composes his self-justificatory propaganda. Self-centered interests, either of hate or of love, are thus at the root of the rebellions, but Basilius's own weaknesses and his misgovernment as king provide ample ground for them to work in. The revolt of the lower orders and also that of Amphialus redound to the discredit of the rebels, but they also reflect severely on Basilius's misconduct. By adding the rebellion of the nobility in *New Arcadia* to the earlier one, which stands alone in *Old Arcadia*, Sidney enlarged his scope for studying the origins and conduct of rebellion, and whatever his plans for bringing it to an end, it is clear that the episode is central to the political concerns of *New Arcadia*. Rebellion in itself constitutes a crisis in political relationships, and Amphialus's defiance of Basilius brings to a head a range of weaknesses and evils that have infected Arcadian life for many years.

As always, however, discussion of Sidney's treatment of rebellion cannot exclude the moral considerations that intermingle with political ones, and among the many significances of the rebellion is that the comparisons and contrasts between Musidorus and Amphialus that were discussed earlier now reach a culmination. The process of establishing the extent of their identity and ultimately of discriminating between them is at its peak in book 3. The two young men fight three times in the course of it, the third fight a most terrible encounter in which both are desperately wounded, though Amphialus has the worst of it. Musidorus's final victory, achieved with much pain and effort, is without doubt a moral victory, and Amphialus, who has succumbed more seriously to the selfish imperatives of uncontrolled desire, has to suffer something near to death before he will be, as may be supposed, reborn in a better state. In dying to old sin and being reborn to fresh virtue, ironically he duplicates the experience of Basilius, the king against whom he so harshly rebels.

While the two young men undergo crucial tests in book 3, Pamela and Philoclea likewise meet theirs. The nature of women and, in particular, the worthiness of women to claim the serious love and devotion of heroes has been a major topic of *New Arcadia* from the beginning. Their worthiness has been affirmed, especially by Pyrocles: now it is to be demonstrated. Pamela's pride and Philoclea's sweetness are to be subjected to intense pressure—moral, psychological, and physical. They are entirely without male support and they do not have the comfort of each other's presence, for they are imprisoned separately. On her own, and calling only on her own resources, each girl has to meet Cecropia's flattery, her blandishments, her arguments, her threats, beatings, torments, and attempts to terrify. Sidney's interest in distinguishing difference in apparent likeness, his subtle perception of shades of character, is nowhere more strikingly evident than here. Given that he wished to show the heroic fortitude of the women, he could have chosen to deal with them as a pair, but he deliberately separates them and gives himself the harder task of individualizing the response that each, according to her own character, makes to the trials imposed upon her. Cecropia, whose own jealous and envious nature will not allow her to see merit in others, thinks the task of interceding with Philoclea on behalf of her son will be no hard matter. Appeals to vanity and the arousal of sexual eagerness seem to her to be guaranteed ways to success, and she conducts her attack with the greatest of skill, waxing lyrical in the course of it about motherhood and the joys of marriage and slipping in praises of Amphialus at strategically telling moments. Much of what she says is well said, and might become a better person than Cecropia; but Philoclea loves Pyrocles, a situation of which Cecropia has no inkling,[33] and Cecropia's persuasions in favour of Amphialus fall on deaf ears or are deflected in Philoclea's mind to apply elsewhere.

In Basilius's siege of Amphialus's stronghold the battle between besiegers and besieged is fought by stages: after an initial pitched battle, there follows a series of individual combats that become progressively more horrifying and bitter as time goes on. So it is with the siege that Cecropia mounts against Pamela and Philoclea. Having failed with her first attack on Philoclea, she tries the same tactics on Pamela, hoping that if she can be won, Amphialus may be willing to transfer his affections to her. Cecropia does not forget that Pamela is the elder sister and "obliquely" touches on "what danger it should be for her if her son should accept Philoclea in marriage and so match the next heir apparent, she being in his power" (NA, 337; P, 465). Pamela, like her sister, has no difficulty in resisting Cecropia's first assaults.

Philoclea's interview with Cecropia is given in detail, whereas Pamela's is summarized, but in the next phase of their ordeal the treatment is reversed. Some time evidently elapses during which Cecropia lets no day pass without renewing her assault on the resolution of the sisters, having decided that, when one is won to be Amphialus's wife, she will poison the other. Foiled once again by Philoclea, she goes to Pamela, and there follows the most serious of all the debates in *New Arcadia* and one that goes to the quick of the book, whether considered as a reflection of and upon life or as a self-contained verbal artifact.

Pamela is working at a piece of embroidery and working at it with great skill and care (NA, 354–55; P, 484). Cecropia notes also that Pamela has dressed herself daintily and taken trouble over her appearance. This gives her hope that Pamela will be more yielding than Philoclea who, in her misery, neglects her appearance; but she is wrong. Pamela's attention to her embroidery and to her appearance are signs not of superficiality but of a noble self-respect that refuses to allow circumstances to force her below her own high standards. As Sidney puts it, "as if it had been her marriage time to affliction, she rather seemed to remember her own worthiness than the unworthiness of her husband" (NA, 355; P, 484). Encouraged to hope that Pamela may be vulnerable through vanity, Cecropia lavishes praises on her work and her beauty, all of which Pamela turns off lightly, conducting her part in the battle of wits with some detachment, almost amusement. But the tone changes when Cecropia begins an attack on what she sees as Pamela's last stronghold, faith in her God. Here the trial of strength between Pamela and Cecropia reaches its climax. Cecropia, like Milton's Comus, has been dealing throughout in "false rules prankt in reason's garb." She has ventured to probe further and further into Pamela's virtue, hoping to find that at some point there is a hollowness through which it can be made to disintegrate. Her attack on divine providence, however, serves not to undermine, as she intends, but, on the contrary, to expose the bedrock on which Pamela's courage and constancy are founded and to show that it is sound. Pamela is no longer content to parry her aunt's attacks with brief but civil speeches. Now she goes on to a fierce attack on her own. Her speech is a very long one and makes a point-by-point refutation of the atheistical arguments at the root of Cecropia's thinking. Since the world of *Arcadia* is a pre-Christian one, Pamela's counterarguments must be drawn from virtuous mind and instinct, not from revelation, and reason it is, she argues, that instructs us in the existence of an "everlasting governor" who works by design. The argument as it develops has deep philosophical roots. Essentially it turns on the distinction between *natura naturans*, the natural world under the control of a beneficent, wise, and providential Designer, and *natura naturata*, a world subject to and deriving from the fortuitous operations of chance.[34] Sidney presents the arguments, through Pamela, with great vigor and decision. He brings out the counterarguments, as he does in his *Apology for Poetry*, in order to demolish them, and, again as in the *Apology*, he enlivens his case with telling imagery. His defense of poetry ends with a mock curse on those who disparage poetry, but Pamela's harangue ends with an utterly serious and grim forecast of damnation: " 'assure thyself, most wicked woman (that has so plaguily a corrupted mind as thou canst not keep thy sickness to thyself, but must most wickedly infect others) . . . that the time will come when thou shalt know that power [God's] by feeling it; when thou shalt see his wisdom in the manifesting thy ugly shamefulness, and shalt only perceive him to have been a creator in thy destruction' " (NA, 363; P, 492).

Pamela's refutation of Cecropia, unrealistic as it may be in the mouth of a young girl, is not out of character. Pamela is as strong-minded and intelligent as Cecropia herself (of Pamela as of her mother it could well be said that "it was happy she took a good course, for otherwise it would have been terrible"). She is always thoughtful and she acts from principles of which she is entirely conscious. In her captivity she more than once invokes her religious faith to sustain her: " 'Well,' said she, 'yet this is the best, and of this I am sure, that howsoever they wrong me, they cannot over-master God,' " and she prays for support in her time of trial (NA, 335–36; P, 463–64). The prayer is a noble and moving one, so much so that if, as may be true, Charles I adopted it on the eve of his execution, there would be no impropriety in this: the words that Sidney gives to Pamela would not be inadequate to the occasion. In *New Arcadia*, Cecropia is lurking at Pamela's door, spying on her as she prays. She hears her words and sees her on her knees and she is daunted by the glimpse of something out of her ken: "even the hard-hearted wicked-ness of Cecropia, if it found not a love of that goodness, yet it felt an abashment at that goodness" (NA, 336; P, 464–65). When Pamela concludes her proof of the existence of an all-knowing God and asserts that in His Justice He will exact final retribution from Cecropia, Cecropia "(like a bat which, though it have eyes to discern that there is a sun, yet hath so evil eyes that it cannot delight in the sun) found a truth but could not love it." She cannot help but feel the impact of Pamela's spiritual fervor, but the impression acts only upon her indurated wickedness to harden her heart yet further.

The importance of this scene in relation to underlying attitudes in *New Arcadia* is obvious enough. The presence of a benevolent and just order sustaining the world gives point and assurance to the trials and tribulations, the exertions and the endurance of heroes and heroines and all who struggle to find their way in the world that Dr Johnson described, using imagery very apt to *New Arcadia*, as a "clouded maze." Spenser also engaged his knights and ladies in dire struggles in the pursuit of virtue, and he too was aware of the need to state a controlling purpose and provide the assurance that all the effort was worthwhile. Nature threatens in many guises in *The Faerie Queene*. Her final manifestation, as we have it, is Mutability in the supposed book 7 and Spenser's answer is to look forward to the time "when no more *Change* shall be." *New Arcadia* is more optimistic. Instead of loathing "this state of life so tickle," Pamela rejoices, even in cap-tivity, in the "goodly work" of the world and finds abundant testi-mony in experience that all things work together, cooperant to an end that is good. In the Pamela-Cecropia encounter, the foundations of goodness, as it is understood in *New Arcadia*, and equally the foundations of evil, are exposed. To that extent the scene constitutes the center of the whole work, as it may indeed have been intended to be at the physical center of the completed text.

The debate with Pamela makes it quite clear that Cecropia is wicked, not merely because she is unscrupulous and violent but because she deliberately persists in evil and repudiates proffered truth. She stands alongside Plexirtus as one of the two major villains of *New Arcadia*, the pair being distinguished from each other in their villainy even as Pamela and Philoclea are in their virtue. Envy, hatred, and greed motivate both Cecropia and Plexirtus, but in Cecropia these evil qualities are combined with love for her son. Plexirtus has a daughter, Zelmane, but no feeling of attachment to her or to anyone else is ascribed to him. He encounters magnanimity but is incapable of being shamed out of his black instincts by it and appears indeed not to acknowledge the existence of purer natures than his own. Cecropia, on the other hand, is capable of being abashed by virtue when she sees it. She has, therefore, grains of potential goodness in her that Plexirtus appears to be utterly without, but she dismisses the insight that Pamela's argument for the existence of a good and just God offers her and reacts by determining the more fiercely to crush what has disconcerted her. Her love for her son, meanwhile, brings him to the very verge of ruin, physical and moral. *New Arcadia* is full of examples of errors, or worse, that stem from sexual passion, but Cecropia's story adds an unexpected twist to all these parables of human frailty. Her love for Amphialus is maternal love, often thought of as most innocent and altrustic, but even that, *New Arcadia* demonstrates, may in a contaminated nature be a source of poison. Amphialus seeks comfort and succor from his mother and she would be willing to give both, but what she offers all but kills him. No human virtue, it would seem, can be relied upon to keep itself sweet unless it is sustained by something beyond itself. Cecropia might have changed her ways by the light that Pamela set before her, but she did not. From that moment, she is not simply one who has gone badly astray but one who is unmitigatedly evil, abandoning even the pretense of kindness, and brutally scourging and tormenting the princesses to terrorize and crush them. Love, loyalty, friendship, family feeling, all take their quality in *New Arcadia* from those who profess them, and those professions in turn rest ultimately on the direction of their lives, whether toward virtue endorsed by a good God or toward destructive evil devoted to the aggrandizement of the self, without conscience or restraint.

Book 3 contains an immense amount of violent action, far more than books 1 and 2, and this action is recorded, so to speak, as it takes place, not retrospectively as so much of book 2's action is. There are intellectual as well as physical confrontations, the Pamela-Cecropia debate not being the only one. Somewhat later, Cecropia demands that Basilius lift the siege or she will kill the princesses and Zelmane (Pyrocles). Kalander counsels surrender to the demand, Philanax counsels against it (NA, 416–18; P, 547–49). Philanax's arguments are intellectually the more impressive, but the scales are tipped in favor of acceding by the sudden entry of Gynecia, "amazed for her daughter Pamela but mad for Zelmane"—she is not concerned about Philoclea since she is her rival for Pyrocles' favor. Basilius, naturally "tender-minded," is easily swayed and agrees to raise the siege "which he saw dangerous to his daughters; but more careful for Zelmane, by whose besieged person the poor old man was straightly besieged." The idea of siege, both literally and metaphorically, is pervasive in book 3, and all the principal actors are driven to crisis points by the pressures it exerts. On this occasion the competing considerations on both sides of the debate are analyzed with the care and subtlety Sidney usually gives to such exercises, but what is of particular interest is that Philanax, shrewd, conscientious, utterly loyal to Basilius as he is, is overruled in argument, not for the first time. He is a rational man who exercises his reasoning powers very efficiently, but human reasoning, Sidney's story insists, is not the measure of all things. Overconfidence in reason made Musidorus naive in his judgments, until he learned to become a more complete man, and reason exercised by the exemplary king Euarchus, in the trial at the end of *Arcadia*, will leave him blind in some areas where he will go astray. Sidney's attitude is not, in any of these instances, a sentimental one. He does not claim that the heart is a better guide than the head, only that men should recognize the limitations of either without the other. Certainly there is little merit in what the hearts of Basilius and Gynecia tell them when Cecropia demands the raising of the siege, for both are prompted by adulterous passion far more than by care for their daughters. But Philanax's head also is in error; he sees well, but not far enough. The point is made explicit when, after the almost-dead body of Amphialus has been borne away by Queen Helen and Anaxius is left in charge, he sends to Basilius for his consent to marry Pamela. Philanax counsels attack on the castle, but Basilius, unable to make up his mind, sends again to consult the Delphic oracle. Philanax is his emissary and is given an answer to his enquiry that is couched for once in plain words, not wrapped in the usual obscurity. Basilius is not to accept Anaxius's proposals, for the princesses are "reserved for such as were better beloved of the Gods." There are other instructions for Basilius and there is also a special message for Philanax himself—that he should "from thence forward . . . give tribute but not oblation to human wisdom" (NA, 457; P, 587). Philanax accepts the lesson, "finding that reason cannot show itself more reasonable than to leave reasoning in things above reason." All this, clearly, relates to the central issue of the Pamela-Cecropia debate. Both Pamela and Cecropia grounded their arguments on reason, but her false trail brought Cecropia to godlessness and "disdainful pride," whereas Pamela's brought her to recognition of a higher power and to humility, as the prayer Cecropia overhears makes plain.

Sidney did not live to complete book 3, but it is evident that he had given strenuous thought and care to its composition. It is designed as the keystone of *New Arcadia*, and it locks into place the divers interests of the whole. Among these is Sidney's interest in the very act he was engaged in as he wrote, the creation of a world out of the material of language. What is said about the Divine Creator and the unity and harmony of His handiwork has evident parallels with the role of the author in relation to his book. The "celestial providence" that directs the affairs of men according to a more comprehensive vision than their own has a counterpart in the author who is the ultimate disposer of the men and women of *Arcadia* and who endorses or rejects the judgments that they make upon each other and upon the situations in which they are involved. Nothing happens by chance, as Pamela tells Cecropia, and her account of the world and its creator is an account also of the book and its author: " 'This world . . . cannot otherwise consist but by a mind of wisdom which governs it; which whether you will allow to be the creator thereof (as undoubtedly he is) or the soul and governor thereof, most certain it is, that whether he govern all, or make all, his power is above either his creatures or his government' " (NA, 362; P, 491). As God makes His world by wisdom and judgment, so Sidney writes his book. "Books," to quote Pamela again, "be but supplies of defects and so are praised because they help our want," and the function of Sidney's book is to provide a model of God's world.[35] By attending to the organization of *New Arcadia* and acknowledging the author's authority, exercised in the service of order for the working out of just ends, the "defects" in human understanding of divine order and harmony are supplied. God and author are twin powers in their respective spheres, and Sidney, giving the full weight of his intelligence to *New Arcadia*, makes the analogy work to render divine intelligence more accessible to the earth-creeping minds of human beings.

Book 3 makes a vital and explicit statement about its world-view and an implicit one about the relation of itself, a work of fiction, to the

Divine Creator; but grand schemes require detailed working. Words have to know their function and fulfil it and stories have to be told as effectively as possible. Whatever metaphysical claims an author may wish to make for the work he or she has in mind, the transference to the page of what Sidney, in the *Apology for Poetry*, calls the "fore-conceit" is a matter of verbal skills. Noone knows this better than Musidorus when he wants to write a letter to Pamela. The purpose he intends for it is clear: it is to obtain some measure of forgiveness for his offense in attempting to embrace her without her consent. The means to attain it are not nearly so clear and involve a desperate and painful struggle with words: "never words more slowly married to-gether . . . fearing how to end before he had resolved how to begin, mistrusting each word, condemning each sentence. This word was not significant, that word was too plain, this would not be conceived, the other would be ill-conceived, here sorrow was not enough ex-pressed, there he seemed too much for his own sake to be sorry, this sentence rather showed art than passion, that sentence rather foolishly passionate than forcibly moving" (NA, 310; P, 437). Kinds of language and their uses were a special interest of Sidney's. He "dare not allow" Spenser's use of rustic language in *The Shepheardes Calendar* because it is not warranted by acceptable precedent,[36] and he writes disparagingly of florid vocabularies both in the *Apology* and in *Astrophil and Stella;* but his concern is not primarily lexical. What fascinates him and engages him in investigation and experiment is the question of how to use words so that they are not simply appropriate individually but that together they are capable of acting upon the sensibilities of a reader and making their message part of his or her experience. This is what Musidorus wants, but he cannot find the words and the order of words adequate to carry the weight of confused emotions that oppress him. His problem is echoed in book 5 of *Old Arcadia* when Pamela also is composing a letter (OA, 397–98; P,828–29). This is to be a plea on behalf of Musidorus to be read at his trial, and like him in the earlier episode, she is intensely conscious of both the power and the limits of the written word. The problem of "read-ership" is also crucial for her, since she does not know how to address the nobles who are holding her prisoner, though she is heir to the throne that now appears to be unoccupied. Her situation raises also, in a quite literal sense, the question of the identity of the author: is she prisoner or is she princess? These questions about the status of her writing occupy her before, having posed them, she turns to specify what her "doleful lines" are intended to "signify" to those who read them. The two letters of the lovers make a pleasing and piquant symmetry, and Sidney may well have meant to keep the second one in revision. That they are composed by Pamela and Musidorus is very appropriate, for these two are intellectual and self-aware and it is fully characteristic of them that they should reflect on the nature of writing at moments when everything depends on what they say and how they say it. "What may words say, or what may words not say?" asks Astrophil in the thirty-fifth sonnet of the sequence, a good question and one that Sidney, like modern students of language, saw as a profound one.

His own method of attempting to answer it is by the employment of many different techniques to make words, if he can, serviceable to his purposes. For some of these purposes there are well-tried and proven formulas at hand. Training in rhetoric gave Sidney the expertise, for example, to render Cecropia's early persuasive addresses to the princesses and the analysis of Basilius's dilemma by Philanax and Kalander. The symbol and emblem-making habits of the Elizabethan imagination gave him the inspiration for pictures such as that of Pamela at prayer (NA, 336; P, 464), and the contemporary theory of the correspondence between the inner world of man and the outer, physical world becomes the basis of an elaborate conceit describing Pamela's embroidery, such as might well have formed a sonnet. To express the appalling wickedness of the scene where Cecropia and her cronies scourge the beautiful body of Philoclea, he similarly calls upon animistic images and on familiar figures from contemporary love poetry (NA, 420; P, 552). The events of book 3—covering a wide range of extremes, which include brutal war, broad farce, and tragic deaths—call for a range of styles to match them. If book 2 is a compendium of narrative methods, book 3 has some claims to be described as a compendium of narrative styles.[37] The death of Argalus, for example, is moving because it is fully in character with what the reader knows of him, and its truth to human feeling makes the last moments painful.

> "My dear, my dear, my better half," he says to Parthenia, "I find I must now leave thee; and by that sweet hand and fair eyes of thine, I swear that death brings nothing with it to grieve me but that I must leave thee, and cannot remain to answer part of thy infinite deserts with being some comfort unto thee." (NA, 378; P, 508)

But Argalus cannot restrain a sigh nevertheless, at the thought of the "disgrace" he has suffered in being defeated in battle. The death of Parthenia, on the other hand, is a much more stylized affair. She appears dressed as a knight, in emblematic armor signifying her grief and mourning. When she is fatally wounded by Amphialus, who does not realize that he is fighting a woman, the red and white and gold, in which the pictures of beautiful and beloved women are so often painted, are composed into a picture of death, not life. Parthenia's helmet falls off, releasing the golden hair that falls over her shoulders. Similar incidents occurring elsewhere (once in *New Arcadia*, see p. 76) are a prelude to love or amity, but not here. Parthenia's complexion is pink and white, but this is "beauty in a new fashion," for the white is partly the pallor of approaching death and the pink has become the deeper red of blood flowing over alabaster skin. Amphialus, seeing this picture of deathly beauty, is "astonished with grief, compassion and shame" and kneels helplessly, begging to be allowed to offer some amends (NA, 398; P, 526–30).

Both scenes contain elements of drama, strong emotions aroused in strong situations with human action and reaction never out of sight, though the style of writing is deliberately varied to keep the reader's responses alert and active. Sidney, in fact, draws increasingly on the mode of drama in the later pages of book 3 to match the immediacy and quick tempo of events as the fate of Amphialus and of the princesses and Pyrocles all hang in the balance. Sidney's response to the theater and what it stands for is a divided one, however, as is apparent in the treatment of the mock executions that Cecropia stages. The nature and purpose of these theatrical scenes are wicked, and the play-acting is here sheerly evil. On the other hand, Sidney exploits with obvious relish the dramatic qualities of theatrical performance to make the kind of impact on his readers he wants. Philoclea is witness of the seeming death of Pamela and, fulfilling herself the role of spectator in a play-within-a-play, she reacts on behalf of the spectator/reader to what is passing before her eyes. The reader's emotions are further stimulated by anxiety about the danger pending to *her*. Pyrocles is the spectator of the second interior drama when he is confronted with the sight of, apparently, Philoclea's severed head. His frenzy makes explicit the state of mind that the reader is being led to, at this moment when it appears that both princesses have been foully murdered. For Pyrocles the death of Philoclea is a personal disaster, but for the reader, who has seen more of the Arcadian world than even Pyrocles has, its significance goes beyond this. The apparent deaths of the princesses cast doubt on what was established in the Pamela/Cecropia debate about the existence and goodness of God. Evil, scotched but not killed, has risen again, it seems, to destroy, and in doing so has called in question the power and the justice of the almighty disposer. "O tyrant heaven! Traitor earth! Blind providence! No justice?" Pyrocles exclaims, "How is this done? How is this suffered? Hath this world a government?" (NA, 431; P, 563). Sidney puts the questions with all the sharpness created by the vivid dramatic representation he has given to the preceding scenes.

The same appreciation of the possibilities of theatrical presentation is in evidence later in the book as theatrical associations continue to accumulate. "Thou playest worse thy comedy than thy tragedy," Pamela tells Anaxius when he unexpectedly and ungraciously becomes a suitor after Amphialus, at death's door, has been carried away from the castle (NA, 454; P, 583); and comedy, surprisingly in the circumstances, becomes a keynote of Anaxius's role. To complement, it appears, the elaborate, quasi-tragic staging of the execution scenes, the story of Anaxius's courtship is played for broad comedy, and Sidney's eye for meaningful gesture or glance is nowhere better illustrated in comic context than in his description, amounting virtually to instructions for an actor, of Anaxius's reception of Pyrocles/ Zelmane's challenge to single combat (NA, 453; P, 582). Beneath the comedy, however, it is never in doubt that Pamela, Philoclea, and Pyrocles are in very grave danger, and the comedy is itself a kind of play-acting over perilous depths, Sidney brilliantly intertwining the two aspects of the situation.

The princesses are themselves brought to play parts in the absurd but threatening wooing of Anaxius and his brothers. Their extreme distaste for any kind of double-dealing, even in situations of the utmost stress, highlights again Sidney's awareness of the moral taint that deception carries with it. Both refuse to connive in Clinias's plans for the murder of Amphialus, and Philoclea rejects Pyrocles' persuasions that she make some show of being ready to accept his suit in order to gain time for rescuing forces to arrive. Yet eventually they do make some concession. Pamela "forces" herself to tell Anaxius to apply to her father for consent to a marriage between them, and both she and Philoclea (and also Pyrocles/Zelmane, who has continually to keep prompting and encouraging them in their show of acceptance) "overpass many insolent indignities of their proud suitors" (NA, 459; P, 589).

The situation and the questions raised by it would interest Bacon. In his essay "Of Simulation and Dissimulation," he deftly sets out moral issues and pragmatic considerations and concludes: "The best composition and temperature is to have openness in fame and opinion; secrecy in habit; dissimulation in seasonable use; and a power to feign if there be no remedy." Sidney examined the whole topic in his own style and his own rather earlier day. Like a man of the world, he recognized the usefulness of both simulation and dissimulation for governors, men of action—and also lovers. With customary honesty, he did not fudge the issues. "Power to feign if there be no remedy" is as far as the princesses can be persuaded to relax their commitment to the truth, and he asks respect and admiration for their conduct. At the same time, it is evident that they have lived secluded lives in which, until now, choices between absolute virtue and practical compromise have not been forced upon them. Pyrocles and Musidorus, on the other hand, have lived in the great world and dealt with men and women who lived by lies, fraud, and manipulation, and they have learned, perforce, to handle the world's weapons, though they have used simulation and dissimulation only in the service of what they believed to be good. Nevertheless they need some correction from the princesses' high-minded rectitude, just as the young women need to learn from Pyrocles that intransigent honesty can in some situations be merely self-destructive folly. In book 3 of *Old Arcadia*, Philoclea makes a bitter reproach to Pyrocles when she thinks that he has deceived her and is now abandoning her (OA, 234–35; P, 686). He is innocent of her charges, but his disguises and duplicity toward others have opened the door to such suspicion. Honesty may not be the best policy in a dishonest world, but those who deal in lies and subterfuge and deceit, however delicately, cannot, at least in *Arcadia*, escape without recognizing some tarnish; yet in an imperfect world, to be whiter than white is impossible and to be flecked with gray is the price, not merely of survival, but of effective action. The moral balance, however, needs to be continually questioned, as it is by Philoclea in this scene and as it will be in the trial later, lest the essential difference between black and white should ever be in danger of being lost in a too easy acceptance of compromise.

Book 3 is an extraordinarily rich composition, containing in concentrated and yet variegated form major elements of Sidney's thinking and of his own character. How he would have concluded it will presumably never be known. Sir William Alexander's bridge passage links the revised text to the continuation in *Old Arcadia*, and it has had its uses in easing the reading of *Arcadia* through the generations. Alexander makes a gallant attempt to imitate Sidney's style and manner but in doing so only highlights how much more intellectual and imaginative power there is in Sidney's own writing and invention. Readers are left with no hope that he wrote with some personal knowledge of what Sidney had in mind. For the rest of *Arcadia*, there is no recourse but to the unrevised text, and how far that can or cannot be aligned with *New Arcadia* is a point to be taken up next.

5
New and Old

New Arcadia breaks off in the middle of a sentence, at a point where an attack (probably led by Musidorus) is about to be launched on Amphialus's stronghold, and within the castle, Pyrocles is engaging Anaxius in deadly combat, having killed his two brothers. William Alexander's bridge passage encompasses the successful conclusion of both fights and restores the two princesses and Pyrocles/Zelmane to the lodges in the forest where they and Basilius and Gynecia resume their former ways as though nothing had happened. This lack of consequence, following the traumatic events of the revised book 3, is the least satisfactory aspect of Alexander's contribution and of the patchwork by which *New Arcadia* is joined to the *Old*. The deficiency is particularly striking in relation to the princesses. Alexander envisages no change in Pamela's behavior from what it was before the soul-searching experiences of the captivity, so that when Musidorus makes himself known after his heroic exertions in rescuing her, according to Alexander she at once reverts to her indignation at his overboldness in attempting to kiss her, an episode long superseded by what has passed since. "How durst you thus presume to present yourself in my presence, being discharged it, when you deserved the uttermost that reason could devise, or fury execute?" she demands. This is merely silly and points to the gap between Alexander's understanding of the book and Sidney's design for it. The princesses have suffered so much, and grown so much, in the course of the revised book 3, that they cannot sensibly be pushed back into a prekidnapping situation, and Sidney would not have wasted the work he had done in book 3 by allowing that to happen.

Alexander's attempt to make a unity of *Old* and *New Arcadia* is plainly a failure, and, being so, it sharpens speculation about what Sidney himself intended to do in the rest of his revision and how far the later developments of the story would have conformed to the original version. The question even arises of whether Alexander's lack of success is symptomatic and indicates that *New Arcadia* has developed in ways impossible to reconcile with anything like the original scheme. According to this line of thought, it was not death that broke off *New Arcadia* but Sidney's despair of being able to finish it; the story lines as he had first laid them down prove incapable of containing what afterward he is trying to cram into them, and he can no longer see a way of controlling the moral issues he has so energetically brought to life: "The revision breaks off in the midst of continuous conflict and chaotic dissolution."[1]

This argument, favored by several recent critics, that the gap between *New Arcadia* and the later parts of the old text is unbridgeable, seems unnecessarily extreme. Sidney had already been amending the *Old Arcadia* version of some later episodes with a view to bringing them into line with the rewriting of the early books, two of these revisions having special relevance to the status of the women characters, a matter that Alexander so conspicuously fails to understand. The first has the effect of removing from Musidorus his intention to take advantage of Pamela's unprotected state during their elopement (OA, 201–2; P, 653–54). The second involves the rewriting of the scene in which Pyrocles visits Philoclea's bedchamber (OA, 228–43; P, 682–90), so that they no longer go so far as to consummate their love. Important as these changes obviously are in relation to the conduct of the heroes, they are no less so in relation to the heroines. When Pyrocles, in a speech to his accusers at his trial, insists on the chastity of Philoclea—"the chaste Philoclea," "the pure Philoclea," "the immaculate Philoclea," "the inviolate Philoclea" (OA, 393; P, 824)—his protestations can be received without any irony. Pamela, likewise, is cleared of any possible suspicion of complicity when Musidorus no longer contemplates breaking his promise of respecting her virginity. The original version of these episodes would certainly have offended against the view of Pamela and Philoclea that has been built up in book 3, and the changes take account of this as well as other considerations arising from the more careful treatment of all the issues in *New Arcadia*.

The revised episodes protect the dignity of the princesses, which has been so much enhanced by their experiences in the revised book 3. One other episode already present in *Old Arcadia* and needing no revision or extension is, as it stands, fully consistent with the developments in the characters of the sisters that have taken place in *New Arcadia*. This is the long debate between Pyrocles and Philoclea about the justification of suicide (OA, 292–300; P, 739–47). It matches Pamela's debate with Cecropia in *New Arcadia*, book 3, in that both give substance to the princesses' virtue by grounding it on a firm and deeply felt faith. It is not mere sentimentality or docility that keeps them good; this is a point, evidently, that was in Sidney's mind even in the first writing of *Arcadia,* and the new book 3, rather than adding a quite new dimension to the princesses, makes more explicit and gives fuller scope to what was already there. In these circumstances it seems unnecessary to assume that the experiences of book 3 would impose radical changes upon the role of the heroines in *Old Arcadia,* books 4 and 5, though some adjustments and perhaps some extensions would probably have been made.

The third alteration, and the longest addition that the 1593 edition makes to the original *Old Arcadia* text, is of a different kind and is striking evidence that Sidney was deliberately sewing together the later developments of *Old Arcadia* with the style and interests of *New Arcadia.* It gives an account of how Euarchus, king of Macedonia, comes to be in Arcadia at the time when Basilius's supposed death, the elopement of Pamela, and the discovery of Pyrocles' sex have thrown the state into chaos. In the original text of *Old Arcadia,* Euarchus (who does not in either version know of these events) has come simply to attempt to reason with Basilius and persuade him to give up his solitary life and resume the care of his kingdom; his absenteeism is damaging to his subjects and exposes the kingdom to the danger of foreign invasion (OA, 357–59). The new, 1593 account is longer and more complicated (P, 787–91). It reintroduces Plangus and tells how he had gone to seek Euarchus, hoping for his help in rescuing Erona from the clutches of Artaxia. Euarchus for some years has been waging war in Byzantium, but before Plangus can reach him there, he hears that the king, having gained victory, has left and returned to Greece to deal with a threat to his own country from the Latins. Sidney then gives a detailed account of how Euarchus prepares to meet this threat, by avoiding provocation of enemies, encouraging potential allies, and meanwhile making careful military preparations in his own territory. The account of Euarchus's behavior makes a pair with the very specific, careful report Sidney gives, in book 3, of how Amphialus acts to safeguard his political and military positions against Basilius after the kidnapping of the princesses. The pairing of these episodes seems to be a major indication that Sidney saw the five books as an essentially unified whole and was working deliberately to integrate them.

An example of a rather different process but with the same tendency occurs in the scene in which Pyrocles faces the rebels surrounding and threatening Basilius's lodge (NA, 284–88; OA, 129–31; P, 382–87). The *New Arcadia* version of this scene, clearly written with much later developments in *Old Arcadia* in mind, includes a passage, not in *Old Arcadia,* that puts in simple, homely terms, adapted to the audience, a defense of constituted authority and the need for patient obedience. The passage makes a specific link with the last books of *Old Arcadia* as Sidney has already written them and in which he has described how, after the supposed death of Basilius, the Arcadian state is on the verge of disintegration, experiencing all the consequences that Pyrocles warns of in cautioning the rustic rioters in the earlier episode. There are defects in all human relationships, Pyrocles tells his audience, but a monarch holds his subjects together and gives them protection from internal and external dangers; it is a weakness of the situation, however, as the events of book 4 further demonstrate, that if the monarch is suddenly removed a state may founder for want of an effective substructure to sustain it (OA, 320–21; P, 766–67). The link between these two passages is evidence of the growth of Sidney's thinking about the scope of *Arcadia* as he was writing the last books of the old version. The political interests that are so strongly in evidence there are further developed in *New Arcadia*, and the insertion in Pyrocles' speech is characteristic of this, as it is also of the technique of anticipation employed predominantly in book 1 but used elsewhere also.

The degree of interaction between the last books of *Old Arcadia* and the incomplete revision is demonstrable in passages such as these, but the influence of one text upon another is not merely a matter of individual correspondences. The treatment of Philanax and Timautus in *Old Arcadia*, book 4, gives advance notice of the technique of comparison and contrast that becomes a major resource of *New Arcadia*. Timautus is a character whom Sidney introduces newly into the story at a very late stage, and he is there specifically to enlarge the range of political reference and analysis by presenting a study of political opportunism. He is "a man of middle age but of extreme ambition" (OA, 321; P, 768) whose interest is solely in exploiting upheaval in the state for his own advantage. The account given of Timautus corresponds to the style of portraits in *New Arcadia*, here, as there, political action and moral quality being inextricably intertwined. The pairing that enables Sidney to make his points effectively is in this instance with Basilius's counselor, Philanax. The different reactions of the two at this demanding moment in Arcadian history bring out the meanness of Timautus and the nobility of Philanax. Philanax is quite free of any ambition to manipulate the crisis in the state to his own advantage, while Timautus is "one that had placed his uttermost good in greatness (thinking small difference by what means he came by it)." The urgent political interests of this part of *Arcadia* are very notable and scarcely prepared for by the first three books of the old text; after the first three books of the revision, however, they seem perfectly natural, according both in matter and manner with the rewriting.

The passages discussed above contribute strongly to the view that the later books of *Old Arcadia* were the inspiration for *New Arcadia* and that the revision was undertaken to provide a more fitting preliminary to the climactic events of books 4 and 5. Precisely by what stages the new thinking evolved and the writing was done is debatable, but in considering how far the composite version can be accepted as essentially, though not formally, a unity, it is vital to take account of the role of Amphialus. The history of Amphialus and his flawed love and contaminated virtue is crucial to the study of male conduct that *New Arcadia* embarks upon from the beginning, and its influence spreads far and wide. The profounder treatment of love and virtue that it typifies necessitates, most importantly, the modifications in the behavior of Pyrocles and Musidorus that Sidney was evidently keen to make in the later books of the *Old Arcadia* text, but its effects are by no means confined to that point. As before, there is a reciprocal action between the older books and the newer ones, notably with respect to the story of Gynecia. Books 3 and 4 raise questions about the individual's moral responsibility that are striking enough in themselves but that, once mooted, Sidney felt the urge to explore further; part of Amphialus's function is to serve as a companion study to Gynecia, of an intrinsically good figure who succumbs to evil promptings even to the extent of imminent moral and physical destruction. Pairings are invariably used by Sidney to discriminate shades of conduct and character ever more finely, and here the comparison of Amphialus and Gynecia acts to deepen the presentation of both. It further substantiates the conclusion that the revision was undertaken to give greater support to the moral and political interests that had developed in the course of composing the later episodes of *Old Arcadia*, and it is also an illustration of how the new writing could bring out more clearly and strikingly the range and implications of all that goes on in *Old Arcadia*, books 4 and 5.

The interrelationship of parts shows clearly that Sidney had by no means discarded the original ending, but, on the contrary, he had books 4 and 5 much in mind as he worked on the revision of books 1, 2, and 3. A study of *New Arcadia* is justified, therefore, in paying careful attention to the later books of the old text, but first, an important point about the moral temper of Sidney's work in both versions needs to be established. It has been a commonplace of some recent criticism that Sidney had a severe and unremitting sense of human sinfulness and that this pervades the writing of *Old Arcadia*. By this account the heroes pursue a career of progressive degradation and Arcadia itself is surveyed with "an extremely jaundiced eye."[2] If this is true of the moral atmosphere of *Old Arcadia*, it must hold true also of *New Arcadia*, for although Sidney changed Pyrocles' and Musidorus's behavior at crucial points, the princes' conduct still gives plenty of ground for suspicion and hostile interpretation. Musidorus still derogates from his position as prince by adopting the dress and status of a shepherd, Pyrocles still dresses up as a woman, and both of them give up their life of princely activity to retreat to a forest and cultivate in some very dubious ways the pursuit of love. Sidney may perhaps have intended that at their trial the charge against them should exclude sexual misconduct and concentrate entirely on murder (from which they are obviously cleared when Basilius revives),[3] but it would still lie as a criticism of their conduct that they have put themselves in a position where guilt might be supposed. If Sidney intended such criticism to reflect a judgment on the innate and ineluctable sinfulness of humanity, a judgment reinforced in his mind as he filled *New Arcadia* with more and more experience of life, he would presumably have found the old ending unacceptable and perhaps yielded up moral questions, and his book, in despair. To take such a view is, however, to underestimate the degree of sophisticated control of his materials that he shows in *New Arcadia*, and it is, moreover, to misunderstand fundamentally Sidney's view of things. To correct this misunderstanding there is no better authority than Fulke Greville. His testimony is rarely given due attention, but it is too important to be passed over and it will be called in evidence now.

Sidney and Greville had known each other since childhood, when they entered Shrewsbury school together on the same day in 1564, both then ten years old. They began court life together in 1575 and traveled together on a diplomatic mission in 1577. Greville was with Sidney when, a few years later, frustrated in his career, he tried to sail with Drake to the West Indies and was recalled by peremptory order of the Queen. He was also a close companion in other pursuits. Two poems by Sidney called "Pastoralls"[4] give an attractive glimpse of three Elizabethan courtiers enjoying each other's company in welcome diversion from the less amicable pursuits of public life. Addressing Fulke Greville and Edward Dyer, a somewhat older man, as "my two," Sidney bids them

> Cause all the mirth you can,
> Since I am now come hether

and he speaks of how they amused themselves by competing in the writing of verses:

> Striving with my Mates in Song,
> Mixing mirth our Songs among.

Greville was out of the country a good deal between 1579 and 1581, but he was an active participant when he was available. He did not spend much time on the endeavors to write English poems in classical meters, which Sidney and Dyer pursued enthusiastically for a time, and he might never have turned to poetry at all but for the influence and example of Sidney. When he did, it was a powerful, mordant, deeply skeptical mind that he had to express, unapt for flights of fancy and exuberant high spirits. "For my own part," he writes years later, remembering the early times, "I found my creeping Genius more fixed upon the Images of Life than the Images of Wit."[5] Some of the poems in Sidney's *Astrophil and Stella* and Greville's *Caelica* read very much as though they were part of the "striving in song" that Sidney refers to, exchanges on similar themes but from different points of view. Sidney, through Astrophil, proclaims romantic ardor; Greville adds an ironic, illusionless commentary.[6]

Greville was not with Sidney when he died, but he was deeply affected by his death. It confirmed that skepticism about the value of this world which he felt even as a very young man, and it led him to invest all his capacity for hope and faith in the absolute values of a world to come. He lived to pursue a worldly career with toughness and some ruthlessness and amassed money and honors, but his mind held always separate the soiled experience of men as he knew it and the purity of the ideal to which humanity is called by Christian teaching. Though Sidney, his first inspiration, was dead, he continued to write poetry, but it moved a long way from the world of *Astrophil and Stella*.

Wealthy and, at some periods, influential as Greville became and long though he lived (he died in 1628), he never forgot Sidney. Indeed, his friend's character and life acquired more and more meaning for him as the years went by, and when finally Greville died, his tomb bore a simple but striking inscription of his own composing: "Fulke Greville, Servant of Queen Elizabeth, Counsellor to King James, Friend to Sir Philip Sidney." The last place given to Sidney here testifies that the friendship was an abiding force to the end, and it suggests also that Greville counted it as his highest honor.

As a friend of long standing and a close associate in Sidney's literary pursuits, Greville's evidence must carry a great deal of weight. As it happens, his connections with *Arcadia* are particularly close. It was to Greville that Sidney entrusted a manuscript of the revision, as far as he had taken it, when he left for the Netherlands in 1585, and it was Greville who felt himself bound to take a particular interest in the fate of *Arcadia* after Sidney's death. When he came to hear of an unauthorized plan to print the book, he wrote in alarm to Sidney's

father-in-law, Sir Francis Walsingham, to warn him. The projected
pirated edition was subsequently stopped, and in 1590 Greville super-
vised the publication of the manuscript in his care. In or around 1610,
he composed an introduction to his own works that, in large measure,
takes the form of a memorial to Sidney and that has consequently
since been known by a shortened version of the title its first editor
gave it in 1652. *The Life of Sidney*, so called,[7] has a good deal to say
about *Arcadia*. As a composition it is imbued with political feeling,
and particularly with Greville's bitterness at what he sees as the
degeneracy of the times in which he is writing, and the misgovernment of England under James. It is not surprising in the circumstances that stress falls on the political interests and lessons contained
in *Arcadia*, but Greville goes beyond that to indicate that Sidney's
purposes were moral in the widest sense. The truth, he states firmly,
is that when Sidney wrote, "both his wit and understanding bent
upon his heart to make himself and others, not in words or opinion,
but in life and action, good and great."[8] Referring specifically to what
he calls "the *Arcadian* Antiques," Greville repeats the point: "his end
in them was not vanishing pleasure alone, but moral images, and
examples, as directing threads, to guide every man through the
confused labyrinth of his own desires, and life."[9]

These comments confirm that serious intentions lie behind the
Arcadian fictions, and Greville also confirms that Sidney was a man of
deep religious feeling: "Above all, he made the Religion he professed, the firm basis of his life," and after his wounding at Zutphen,
when he realized that he was not going to recover, he prepared
himself earnestly by prayer and instruction for death. All this Greville
testifies to; what he does not say is that *Arcadia* is a Calvinist tract,
obsessed with the sinfulness of the world, gloomy and near despair
about the depraved state of man. On the contrary, *Arcadia* makes
evidently too many concessions to sheer enjoyment for Greville's
more saturnine nature to be entirely comfortable with it. It is a
"various and dainty" work, he says, but no more than marginal
decoration to Sidney's more serious literary tasks, such as his translation of the work, *On the Trewnes of the Christian Religion*, by the French
Huguenot Phillipe du Plessis Mornay, or his translations of the
psalms. The revised *Arcadia* is superior to the older version, and
Greville likes the work too much, as he puts it, "to condescend that
such delicate, though inferior, pictures of himself should be sup-
pressed"[10] but inferior, in his judgment, they undoubtedly are "scrib-
bled rather as pamphlets for entertainment of time and friends than
any account of himself to the world."[11] As for Sidney's casting a
"jaundiced eye" on the world and humanity within it, Greville ap-

pears to have noticed no such thing, for he describes Pyrocles and Musidorus as, unequivocally, "the two excellent Princes" and speaks of Sidney himself as "such a lover of mankind, and goodness" that he offered "comfort, participation and protection to the uttermost of his power" wherever he found talent and merit. His sympathies were wide, not confined only to those whose interests and activities ran along the same lines as his own, for "his heart, and capacity were so large, that there was not a cunning painter, a skilful engineer, an excellent musician, or any other artificer of extraordinary fame, that made not himself known to this famous spirit and found him his true friend without hire; and the common rendezvous of worth in his time."[12] This is a picture of a positive man, enthusiastic and responsive, one who sought out and rejoiced in the achievements of his fellow men and nourished "goodness" wherever he found it. It tells strongly against those who argue otherwise.

On his deathbed Sidney ordered that *Arcadia* should be destroyed. It was a work, Greville says, "rich (like his youth) in the freedom of affections, wit, learning, style, form, and facility, to please others," but in his suffering, as the surgeons probed and his body grew weaker and gangrene set in, "he then discovered, not only the imperfection, but the vanity, of these shadows, how daintily soever limned: as seeing that even beauty itself, in all earthly complexions, was more apt to allure men to evil than to fashion any goodness in them."[13] Sidney's experiences in Holland had greatly depressed him. As he lay dying with, it would seem, all his promise and hopes unfulfilled, it is scarcely surprising that he should want to discard a fiction that breathed of youth and energy and hope and that it now appeared a vanity. It was, besides, unfinished, a point that Greville stresses. If he did not wish this imperfect work to survive him, that again is entirely understandable, but there is no warrant for reading the world-weariness of his deathbed back into *Arcadia* and the time of its composition.

Greville's cast of mind was always more somber than Sidney's, and when he wrote the *Life* he was more than twenty years older than his friend had been when he died. He had seen much to confirm the skepticism with which he confronted Sidney's enthusiasm when they were both young. He "knew the world," as he wrote of himself, a necessary knowledge but not, to his mind, one to be proud of; and he "believed in God," a belief that held the possibility of damnation always before his eyes. *Arcadia* is too light-hearted for his taste, and he writes as though to persuade his reader that Sidney would have weighted it more had he lived to finish it. Perhaps if Sidney had lived to Greville's age he would, but then it would have been a different

book, reflecting a much changed character. Greville forgets that the
Sidney who wrote *Arcadia* was the young man who "mixed mirth"
with his writing, as the "Pastoralls" say, and who told his friends to be
prepared to be jolly because he was coming to join them; but his
reservations about *Arcadia* only serve to make it clear beyond doubt
that for this man, who really did take a grim view of the world and
human activity within it, *Arcadia* was not a book that embodied his
views.

What Greville says and does not say is equally significant in relation
to *Astrophil and Stella*, which has received the same sort of puritanical
attention from critics in recent years. Greville makes no mention of
the sonnet sequence at all, presumably because he thought of it as a
youthful folly, disqualified for the attention he gives, albeit with some
reluctance, to *Arcadia*, by its lack of political and ethical matter.
There have been a number of attempts of late to treat these poems
like *Arcadia*, as a cautionary tale of moral deterioration, with Astrophil
fulfilling the role ascribed to Pyrocles and Musidorus;[14] but those who
pursue this line need again to reckon with Greville. He did not see
Sidney's poems as a moral parable at the time—quite the contrary, as
his companion poems show—and he did not claim them as such with
hindsight. His own sequence, *Caelica*, moves away from the vagaries
of human love to passionate meditation on God and human sin.
Astrophil and Stella makes wry acknowledgment of the weaknesses of
the flesh and dramatizes the tension between human longing and
moral and social law, but Sidney does not resolve the tensions by
rejection of the world and human love.

> Oh wearisome condition of humanity!
> Born under one law, to another bound:
> Vainly begot, and yet forbidden vanity,
> Created sick, commanded to be sound:
> What meaneth nature by these divers laws?

So writes Greville in a fierce and splendid chorus to his play *Mustapha*.
Sidney's tone is different. When he was a young man, not yet twenty,
Languet wrote him a letter in which he gently reproached him for
what he thought an oversevere judgment on the author of a defense of
the St. Bartholomew's Day massacre, an event that had occurred
when Sidney was in Paris and that had, naturally, appalled him. The
writer of the defense had been under threat of death for showing
sympathy with Protestants, Languet explains, and he goes on: "I am
accustomed to judge of men otherwise than most persons do; unless

they are utterly depraved (for I do not think *such* men's vices ought to be concealed), I cull out their good qualities if they have any; and if through error or weakness they fail in any point, I put it out of sight as far as I can."[15] This seems to have been a lesson Sidney took to heart. What in *Arcadia* he calls "contradictions growing in those minds which neither absolutely climb the rock of virtue nor freely sink into the sea of vanity" (NA, 232; P, 329), move him to sympathy, not to condemnation. Like Languet, he rejects only those who prove themselves without doubt to be utterly depraved. *Old Arcadia* and *New Arcadia* alike demonstrate this attitude, *New Arcadia* even more clearly than the *Old* because of the amplification of what is only sketched or left unclear in the earlier text; but the treatment of the final episodes of *Old Arcadia* sets the tone, in this respect as in others, for the fuller and more deeply worked revision and need not, therefore, have been essentially changed if Sidney had lived to complete his book.

Part and parcel of Sidney's sympathetic and humane view of the difficulties of the well-disposed man or woman struggling to be good in a bewildering world is his sense of humor. It is as prominent as his sense of sin and serves to mitigate it. There is comedy in *Astrophil and Stella*, much gentle irony and amusement in the *Apology for Poetry*, and comedy everywhere in both versions of *Arcadia*. *New Arcadia* is the product of serious thought and powerful motivation to embody the results of that thinking in fiction, but it contains a larger comic element than *Old Arcadia*. The episode of Dametas's fight with Clinias is added in the new book 3 (NA, 380–85; P, 509–16), an incident of rumbustious fun, a farcical parody of the knightly challenges and encounters surrounding it. The fight between two reluctant and ill-qualified combatants is reminiscent of the Viola-Aguecheek duel in *Twelfth Night*, and Shakespeare perhaps owed the idea to Sidney. Dametas and Clinias are coarser characters than Shakespeare's timid pair, and the comedy is more robust too, but there are delightful touches of other kinds. Dametas's impenetrable stupidity makes a serious point against Basilius who chooses to put trust in such a man, and Clinias's meanness of spirit makes him a real danger, but the roles he gives them elsewhere do not inhibit Sidney from deriving a good deal of evident enjoyment from imagining in detail the various stages of their ridiculous combat.

Amusement of a subtler kind manifests itself on all sorts of occasions, a particularly interesting example being the debate about love between Pyrocles and Musidorus in book 1, which occurs in both *Old* and *New Arcadia*. A serious breach between the two young men is threatened there, but Sidney brings the episode to a conclusion in laughter. The argument has been driven to a point at which they are both shocked into silence at the gulf that has opened at their feet:

> And thus remained they a time, till at length Musidorus, embracing him [Pyrocles], said "And will you thus shake off your friend?"
>
> "It is you that shake me off," said Pyrocles, "being for my unperfectness unworthy of your friendship."
>
> "But this," said Musidorus, "shows you more unperfect, to be cruel to him that submits himself unto you. But since you are unperfect," said he, smiling, "it is reason you be governed by us wise and perfect men."

Musidorus then proceeds to give instructions to Pyrocles, including one that he should love Philoclea with "all the powers of [his] mind" (NA, 77; OA, 25; P, 139). Pyrocles' countenance brightens at once. His "heart was not so oppressed with the two mighty passions of love and unkindness but that it yielded to some mirth at this commandment of Musidorus that he should love." The laughter does not diminish the seriousness of the issues that have been debated nor the sincerity of the two young men. It does, however, indicate that argument can get out of hand and that intellectual positions rigidly held can lead to destructive conclusions. The debate shows Musidorus in some danger of being a prig, but he is saved by the smile with which he dissolves the quarrel with his friend. His Arcadian experiences will teach him that human affairs are not to be so neatly summed up as in the rhetorical wisdom he has been so eager to display to Pyrocles, and he will be able to accept the lesson. If Musidorus is intellectually austere, Pyrocles' sensibility may be overemotional, but he also is saved by being able to see the irony of the situation and laugh at it. Laughter is the signal that gives hope for the healthy development of both their natures. Its presence in *Arcadia* as a whole is also a sign of poise in the author.[16] So much in control is he of his own skills in managing his book and so confident in the control of a provident God in managing His world, that he can afford to see the comedy and laugh at the ironies of human behavior. There is nothing frivolous in this, and paradoxically, the presence of humor in the book is one of the strongest reasons for taking *Arcadia* seriously.

It is also another argument against narrowly moralistic readings and strengthens the case for the unity of tone in *Old* and *New Arcadia*.

6
Trial and Human Error

That the two aspects of human experience, comic and tragic, lie close to each other is a perception that produces some of Shakespeare's most powerful scenes, and though Sidney has nothing like the heath scene in *King Lear,* he too knows that a situation can be at the same time both tragic and comic. He switches moods, sometimes he fuses them, and he plays along the range of irony from the farcical to the deadly serious. Book 4 begins, for example, with ludicrous episodes involving Dametas, Miso, and Mopsa, which sketch in the broadest terms the follies and dangers arising from credulity and intentions misunderstood. The following episode, in which Basilius and Gynecia unintentionally spend a night together in a cave, turns on the same point and has all the elements of a witty comedy, but at the end of the scene, death and the anguish of bitter remorse enter and the comedy turns into threatened disaster. From that point on the ironic contrasts between expectation and event, which have been matter for amusement in the opening pages of book 4, are no longer funny. They become, instead, a means of deep and painful probing of character and intent.

The story of Basilius's and Gynecia's night in the cave concentrates an eventful moral history. Gynecia expected to embrace Pyrocles, but it is her husband who comes to her instead. He believes he is embracing the Amazon, Zelmane, and rhapsodizes on the joys he has experienced. Daylight reveals his wife to him and floods him with confusion. She, who has been under no illusion from the moment he climbed into bed beside her, now addresses him in terms of great dignity and magnanimity: "Truly, truly, Sir, very untimely are these fires in you. It is time for us both to let reason enjoy his due sovereignty. Let us not plant anew those weeds which by nature's course are content to fade" (OA, 277; P, 727). Her words entirely belie her state of mind, which is, in fact, a compound of guilt on her own account and "spiteful doubt" that she has been tricked by Pyrocles, but Basilius is quite overcome by the appearance of nobility and his wife's "unexpected mildness." Her hypocrisy acts upon him like the genuine article, and he repents of his misconduct and vows amendment.

Both Basilius and Gynecia have believed that they are cleverly manipulating events for their own ends, and both are deceived. Their intentions have been sinful, and by no will of their own they are saved from fulfilling them; but, far from ending on a note of satisfaction, the scene appears to lead to stark tragedy. Basilius has drunk from the cup that Gynecia prepared for Pyrocles and that she believed contained a love philter. He at once shows symptoms of having been poisoned, and he falls to the ground, apparently dead. Gynecia, horrified, attempts to revive him but without success. In the shock of his death, guilt and remorse and shame overwhelm her and she sees her own conduct of the recent past in a clear and merciless light:

> Her painful memory had straight filled her with the true shapes of all the fore-past mischiefs: her reason began to cry out against the filthy rebellion of sinful sense, and to tear itself with anguish for having made so weak a resistance: her conscience, a terrible witness of the inward wickedness, still nourishing this debateful fire; her complaint now not having an end to be directed unto, something to disburthen sorrow, but a necessary down-fall of inward wretchedness. (OA, 279; P, 729)

Thus, by ironies that cut in several directions, Basilius and Gynecia are both brought to extremity and Gynecia will be tried for the murder of her husband.

At her trial her principal accuser is Philanax, and he himself becomes an object of close and extensive study in books 4 and 5. Like other characters, he is on trial in the final emergency in *Arcadia*. Throughout the earlier pages, he has been notable for his objective analysis of the problems put to him and has appeared as a man of admirable stability. In the crisis that comes upon Arcadia—the King apparently dead, the Queen accused of his murder, the heir to the throne arrested together with her sister, both of them having been caught in compromising circumstances with young men who have been living in disguise and are now suspected of having planned regicide and usurpation—Philanx is tested to the utmost. In a political context he has been presented throughout as a model of probity and unselfish devotion to duty, a fact highlighted by the contrast with Timautus; on a more personal level, however, it now becomes apparent that he is not by any means beyond blame. He has been most deeply attached to Basilius, and his insistence that justice be done on the King's murderers is fired with a fierce desire for revenge. His heart is quite hardened toward Gynecia, and he looks on her with "vindicative resolution in his face" and "transported with an unjust justice, that his eyes were sufficient heralds for him to denounce a mortal hatred" (OA, 287; P, 735). He behaves with real cruelty to Dametas and his family, punishing them, it would seem, not only for their own follies but also because of Basilius's foolish confidence in his herdsman, which has been a cause of exasperation to himself. His hatred of the accused princes knows no bounds, and he is determined that nothing shall stand in the way of their condemnation. So that no evidence shall be heard to mitigate their supposed crimes, he suppresses the letters that the princesses compose to be read in court, though he has no shadow of right to do so. He opens the letters, but seeing their tendency, "he would not himself read them over, doubting his own heart might be mollified, so bent upon revenge" (OA, 398, P, 829). His speeches for the prosecution are of the utmost virulence, and here comes one of Sidney's telling ironies, for Philanax's mode of forensic oratory has already been condemned by Philanax himself. At an earlier stage of the crisis, Timautus, jealous of Philanax's authority and anxious to undermine it, has made a very clever speech designed to discredit Philanax in the eyes of the powerful men of the state. With great plausibility and rhetorical skill he systematically misrepresents all Philanax's actions and intentions in the measures he is taking to bring a dangerous situation under control. Philanax's thoughtful reply goes with characteristic acuteness to the heart of the matter:

> "My lords," he says, "let not Timautus' railing speech (who, whatsoever he finds evil in his own soul, can with ease lay it upon another) make me lose your good favour. Consider that all well doing stands so in the middle betwixt his two contrary evils that it is a ready matter to cast a slanderous shade upon the most approved virtues." (OA, 324; P, 770)

When his emotions are not engaged, Philanax sees clearly and acts honorably, but he forgets his own words when his passions are stirred, as they are by the apparent death of Basilius. Reason is not in itself an infallible guide to wisdom, as the oracle has admonished him, but much less is the rabid thirst for vengeance with which Philanax pursues those whom he takes to be Basilius's murderers. Under its influence he ceases to weigh evidence dispassionately and even suppresses testimony that might make against his prejudged conclusion. Though he claims to act for justice, malice, spite, and venom color all he says and he takes the "ready way to cast a slanderous shade" on all that the Queen and princes have done. He has hitherto behaved immaculately, according to his perhaps somewhat confined sense of right and wrong, but he now behaves very badly; if the princes are to be condemned out of his mouth, this will clearly be a miscarriage of justice.

Judgment and sentence lie ultimately not with Philanax, however, but with Euarchus, and Sidney lays great emphasis on Euarchus's reputation as a just judge. That Euarchus condemns Pyrocles and Musidorus and persists in their condemnation even when he discovers that they are his own son and nephew must, on the face of it, weigh heavily against them. Yet Sidney's presentation of the whole situation, considered with the care that its thoughtfulness and subtlety deserve, should dispose of any assumption that the issues are clear-cut and that Euarchus penetrates to the truth of things. There are, in fact, many flaws in Euarchus's conduct. He begins by accepting Pyrocles' account of his nighttime visit to Philoclea and, in her absence, "finding by his wisdom that she was not altogether fault-less," pronounces that she will be confined for the rest of her life among religious women and strictly vowed to chastity. All this, as Pyrocles realizes, is "a great prejudicating of his own case" (OA, 381; P, 812), but his major concern is to protect the princess and he rejoices that he has saved her from worse blame. Euarchus then accepts Gynecia's false confession that she was indeed Basilius's murderer and sentences her to death. This is plain error, as more sensitive observation and understanding might have shown, and Pyrocles takes time from his own defense to draw attention to this defi-ciency in Euarchus (OA, 393–49; P, 825). Pyrocles knows no more than Euarchus of what really happened in the cave, but he makes a juster assessment of Gynecia and her behavior than the judge. Eu-archus upholds the law and, in judging, considers himself limited by it; but the application of "dead pitiless laws," as Philanax speaking to Philoclea calls them (OA, 304; P, 752), though it may provide a salutary discipline, is of its nature a limited exercise.

Sidney makes his own opinion on this point quite clear in his *Apology for Poetry*. He is considering which among the candidates for the honor of being the most effective teacher of virtue should bear the palm. He decides for poetry, and on the way he dismisses any claims the lawyer may have:

> for the lawyer, though *jus* be the daughter of justice, and justice the chief of virtues, yet because he seeketh to make men good rather *formidine poenae* than *virtutis amore;* or, to say righter, doth not endeavour to make men good, but that their evil hurt not others; having no care, so he be a good citizen, how bad a man he be; therefore as our wickedness maketh him necessary, and necessity maketh him honourable, so is he not in the

deepest truth to stand in rank with these who all endeavour to take naughtiness away and plant goodness even in the secretest cabinet of our souls.[1]

Euarchus, as a good and honorable administrator of justice, has the strengths and weaknesses of Sidney's lawyer. His concern is not with the quality of character of those he tries, but his emphasis lies particularly on their duties as subjects and citizens and the disruptive effects their actions may have on the body politic.[2] He judges Gynecia guilty of the murder of her husband, a private offense but, even worse, a public one because her husband was king. Pyrocles and Musidorus have attempted to rob Basilius, as father, of his daughters, but their attempt is all the more to be abominated because Pamela and Philoclea are "prince's children, where one steals, as it were, the whole state and well-being of that people" (OA, 406; P, 837). To admit excuses for their conduct would be "to palliate such committed disorders as to the public shall not only be inconvenient but pestilent" (OA, 407; P, 838).

To say of Euarchus that he does not care how bad a man may be so long as he is a good citizen would be unfair, but it is nevertheless true that his role as judge is presented as a circumscribed one and he makes no attempt to go beyond it. When he finds that he has condemned his son and nephew and knows that these prisoners, on whom Philanax has been allowed freely to pour abuse, are young men who have shown themselves to be greatly endowed with natural gifts and have "to the wonder of the world heretofore behaved themselves as might give just cause to the greatest hopes that in an excellent youth may be conceived" (OA, 411; P, 841), he yet cannot find grounds to reassess the case. The law may be an ass in Arcadia as elsewhere.[3]

Euarchus is an intelligent, honorable, and deeply conscientious man. Nevertheless, he delivers verdicts that must be overturned because they fail to do true justice. They are overturned by a man who does not at all qualify for the adjectives applied to Euarchus, but the resurrected Basilius takes all things for the best and reinterprets those events, which to Euarchus and Philanax have been black and sinister, in terms, not of crime and punishment but of love and honor, "considering all had fallen out by the highest providence and withal weighing in all these matters his own fault had been the greatest" (OA, 416; P, 846). The letter of the law would have killed, but the spirit of thankfulness and humility and reconciliation gives life. The ironies implicit in all these events scarcely need pointing out. Euarchus acts from law and conscience but would commit unwarranted destruction. Philanax acts, as he thinks, from justice but in malice and spite seeks revenge. Gynecia prosecutes herself for a crime she has not committed and is in the end honored for an unstained virtue to which, in fact, she can hardly lay claim. The princes, who have been patterns of heroism and sought to pursue honorable love, stand accused of murder, seduction, and the intention to subvert the state, and they are condemned to death by a man who is bound by kinship and affection to love and protect them. The disparity between what they intended and what has transpired strikes Musidorus:

> "Alas," he says to Pamela, "how contrary an end have all the inclinations of my mind taken! My faith falls out treason unto you and the true honour I bear you is the field wherein your dishonour is like to be sown. But," he goes on, "I invoke that universal and only wisdom (which examining the depth of hearts, hath not his judgment fixed upon the event). . . ." (OA, 311, P, 757)

These are important words, for they offer the key to the implications of the trial scene and its denouement. As Sidney sees them, human beings are inevitably subject to delusion and error, about themselves and about others, and even the justest man, or the noblest, needs help from resources other than his own if he is to be saved when he finds that, by his own fault or that of others, his intentions are twisted to ends that are entirely the opposite of what he sought. What these resources are touches a number of important issues, among them the question of the significance of the temporal setting of *Arcadia*.

Pyrocles and Musidorus, however intrinsically virtuous they and their princesses may be, are pagans living in a pre-Christian world. Sidney does not himself apply to them words like "salvation" and "redemption," and writing as a Christian in a society that was keenly alive to theological thinking, he is aware of the large question mark hanging over the status of virtuous pagans. How seriously he was interested in this matter is evidenced by the fact, reported by Greville, that as he lay dying, slowly and in great pain, he entreated the ministers who attended him "to deliver the opinion of the ancient heathen touching the immortality of the soul, first, to see what true knowledge she retains of her own essence, out of the light of herself; then, to parallel with it the most pregnant authorities of the Old, and New Testament, as supernatural revelations, sealed up from our flesh for the divine light of faith to reveal and work by."[4] His anxiety in extremity to have recalled to him what "the ancient heathen" had had to say confirms what both versions of *Arcadia* would in any case make plain, that the extent and validity of pagan religious enlightenment was a matter to which he gave considerable thought. Articles 13 and 18 of the 39 Articles of the Church of England take a hard Calvinist line on the subject, but not everyone, even among devout Protestants, accepted this view. Sidney's friend Du Plessis Mornay did not,[5] and it would be an insupportable irony if the creator of Pyrocles, Philoclea, and the rest, who brought them through many trials to a haven of love, forgiveness, and unity at the end of his book, were to have in his mind that really they were all destined to everlasting perdition. It might be argued that since this is only a fiction Sidney was not bound to pursue such matters to their ultimate and that the pastoral setting gave him liberty to take up religious topics—a traditional use of pastoral—and to drop them again whenever it suited, but, in fact, the treatment of religion is too sustained and serious in later books for such an idea to be sustainable.

The debate between Pamela and Cecropia about evidence for the existence of a benevolent God has already been discussed. It occurs only in *New Arcadia*, but as with other aspects of the revision, the seeds for it are sown in books 4 and 5 of *Old Arcadia*. Early in book 4, Dametas finds "Zelmane," the supposed Amazon, asleep with Philoclea in her bedroom and at the same time sees that the Amazon is in fact a man. Soon after, Pyrocles wakes and realizes that his secret has been discovered and that he and Philoclea are now in grave danger. His concern is for Philoclea, and it seems to him that the only chance there is of protecting her reputation and saving her from Arcadian law, which will assume she is unchaste and condemn her accordingly, is for him to take his own life. He wrenches an iron bar from the window with which to kill himself, but the blow he gives fails to do this. He is, however, badly bruised, and the noise of his fall wakes Philoclea. Then follows a debate between them, in which Pyrocles maintains the right to take his own life in order to save hers, and Philoclea marshals counterarguments to dissuade him. Pyrocles speaks throughout with a cool rationality and the lofty unconcern for bodily pain of the Stoic philosophers. Philoclea counters with the argument that suicide springs from cowardice, not from courage; "Whatsoever . . . comes out of despair cannot bear the title of valour, which should be lifted up to such a height that, holding all things under itself, it should be able to maintain his greatness even in the midst of miseries" (OA, 294; P, 742). This itself is a Stoic thought, matching the ideal of high-minded self-control that Pyrocles is representing, but it is also close to Christian teaching of submission to the will of God. Philoclea's use of the word "despair" itself suggests Christian resonances. She goes on to argue that "it is not for us to appoint that mighty majesty what time he will help us; the uttermost instant is scope enough for him to revoke everything to one's own desire. And therefore to prejudicate his determination is but a doubt of goodness in him who is nothing but goodness" (OA, 297; P, 745). At this point Stoicism modulates into intuition of a God to whose will man must at all times submit but that he must not presume to foreknow, trusting always in the divine goodness. Pyrocles has "a judicial habit of virtue," which gives him nobility of mind, but Philoclea has "a simple voidness of evil" (OA, 294; P, 741) leading her beyond Stoicism to an awareness of God that approaches very near to the Christian.

What the heathen philosophers had to say about the afterlife was in Sidney's mind as he lay dying, and this also is a subject that arises in *Arcadia*. Philanax makes a general reference to "the eternal mansion" that he believes Basilius, dead, possesses (OA, 286; P, 734), but this is hardly significant. Much more important is part of the discussion that Pyrocles and Musidorus have with each other as, in expectation of imminent death, they review their lives during their imprisonment. Their talk turns to the question of whether they will retain memory after death. Musidorus reminds his friend that "it is greatly held" that, with the death of the physical faculties, memory must also be lost, and "then is there left nothing but the intellectual part or intelligence which . . . doth only live in the contemplative virtue and power of the omnipotent good, the soul of souls and universal life of this great work" (OA, 372; P, 804). Pyrocles' reply is presented as his own personal thinking[6] and is an argument, developed at some length, that memory will persist, though of a different nature from that of the living, which belongs to the world of the senses, and that he and Musidorus will retain knowledge of their friendship in the afterlife. This goes within a hair's breadth of the Christian doctrine of personal immortality, and Sidney's treatment of Pyrocles' speech seems to show a "virtuous pagan" straining by the light of innate virtue and strenuous thought to the boundaries of Christian revelation.

Christian thought lies in the background of *Arcadia*, just beyond the reach of the characters. Their strivings toward it, however, are of great significance in relation to Sidney's view of human nature, for they show an innate disposition to virtue and a thirst for divine love. Sidney finds much propensity to good in humanity, together with its manifold weaknesses. His own faith is given to a God who teaches that forgiveness should extend to offenses multiplied even seventy times seven.

Changes made in the first sentence of book 4 are revealing in this and other connections. They show Sidney increasingly clarifying his thought as he works on his text, and they also indicate clearly in what direction his thinking tended. To follow this direction is to see how he came to understand the meaning of vice and virtue, rejection and salvation. The first sentence reads as follows:

> The everlasting justice (using ourselves to be the punishers of our faults, and making our own actions the beginning of our chastisement, that our shame may be the more manifest, and our repentance follow the sooner) took Dametas at this present (by whose folly the others' wisdom might receive the greater overthrow) to be the instrument of revealing the secretest cunning—so evil a ground doth evil stand upon, and so manifest it is that nothing remains strongly but that which hath the good foundation of goodness. (OA, 265)

Sidney revised this, and in the 1593 edition the sentence reads:

> The almighty wisdom (evermore delighting to show the world that by unlikeliest means greatest matters may come to conclusion, that human reason may be the more humbled and more willingly give place to divine providence) as at the first it brought in Dametas to play a part in this royal pageant, so having continued him still an actor, now that all things were grown ripe for an end, made his folly the instrument of revealing that which far greater cunning had sought to conceal. (P, 715)

The changes involved here are unobtrusive but important. They provide another example, to add to others, of how, though he had not yet completed Book Three, Sidney was looking ahead to the later Books and making significant adjustments of tone and language to bring them into line with his revision.[7]

The change from "everlasting judgement" to "almighty wisdom" signals a shift of emphasis. Chastisement and shame are now replaced by stress on the limitations of human reason and the need to depend upon "divine providence," a point that is characteristic of *New Arcadia* and that books 4 and 5 reinforce. The language of the 1593 sentence is also notably less severe than it was in the original. When Sidney wrote the first version, he evidently wanted to make it plain that the time had come for a serious accounting by the characters for their actions, and the repeated word "evil" strikes a heavy and ominous note; but this is puzzling, for *Old Arcadia* so far has not established a context in which either "evil," or "goodness" with which it is contrasted, can have a distinct meaning. In writing *New Arcadia* Sidney was giving himself much more space to work out this kind of question, and as he mined further into the ground of his original story and explored more and more of its extent and implications, the first formulation of the sentence must have seemed careless and even crude. Evil and goodness admit of many degrees, as plentiful stories in *New Arcadia* illustrate. The various discriminations that have taken place across an extensive spectrum of moral attitude and behavior and that continue to take place in the trial itself and its preliminaries forbid the casual use of such words as "evil" and "goodness." When he first wrote the sentence, Sidney may have had in mind Musidorus's frustrated attempt on Pamela and Pyrocles' lovemaking, and he may not have anticipated at how deep a level he would become engaged with the events that were still to come. The pressure put on his principal characters by these events leads him into probings and discoveries to which the original version of the first sentence by no means does justice. By the time he rewrote it, he had conceived the characters of Cecropia and Plexirtus, and with them the true dimensions of evil become clear.

Both of them are hardened sinners. The particular forms of their villainy differ but they are equally obdurate. Plexirtus, a bastard son, is a coldhearted murderer and hypocrite who is twice saved from a deserved death by the filial piety of others: once by his half-brother, Leonatus, who for the sake of their common father forgives him multiple acts of treachery; and again by his own daughter, Zelmane, who pleads with Pyrocles to rescue him, at great risk, when he has been made captive and is threatened with a hideous death. This rescue seems actually to be effective in bringing Plexirtus to a better way of life. He is among the many great persons and princes who assemble to manifest their gratitude to and admiration for Musidorus and Pyrocles when the young princes leave Asia Minor and set sail for Greece. It is Plexirtus who provides the ship and who so behaves that the young men "now not only forgave but began to favour [him], persuading ourselves with a youthful credility that perchance things were not so evil as we took them and, as it were, desiring our own memory that it might be so" (NA, 272; P, 371). In fact it is not so, as the princes discover when one of Plexirtus's chief counselors, who is sailing with them, reveals to them that Plexirtus has plotted to have them murdered before they get to Greece. The counselor has been converted from his evil allegiance by his experience of the "excellencies' (NA, 273; P, 372) of the princes while they are in his company on board ship. He does his best to protect them when the captain, who "with a loud voice sware that if Plexirtus bade him, he would not stick to kill God himself," stirs up the crew to attack them.

Plexirtus is an example of the "inward atheist" or Machiavellian hypocrite[8] who conceals his real contempt for all moral and religious law under a fiction of corrigibility, always promising, never intending, amendment. He is terribly dangerous. He trades on the virtue of the good, while being himself a secret agent of violence and blackest corruption. The fight that takes place on board the ship carrying Pyrocles and Musidorus to Greece typifies the evil that he does and the moral confusion he spreads around him. Some of the crew, under the leadership of the captain, fight to kill the princes; others follow the lead of the counselor and fight to protect them. " 'The narrowness of the place,' Pyrocles tells Philoclea, 'the darkness of the time [it was night] and the uncertainty in such a tumult how to know friends from foes'" made decisive action impossible: " 'I think we never performed less in any place,'" he goes on, " '. . . for not discerning perfectly who were for or against us, we thought it less evil to spare a foe than spoil a friend'" (NA, 274; P, 373). This is the principle on which Plexirtus's own life has been saved, by the scrupulous and benevolent, but their mercy only gives him the occasion to rob others of life. The counselor is killed on the ship, together with almost everyone else. Then fire breaks out and the few who are still alive unite, perforce, in an unsuccessful attempt to save the ship. This becomes the shipwreck whose aftermath forms the opening episode of *New Arcadia*.

There are three shipwrecks in *New Arcadia*—this, another when the princes, at the beginning of their adventures, sail to join Euarchus at Byzantium (NA, 165–68; P, 261–64), and that which befalls Euarchus himself and brings him to Arcadia at the time of Basilius's supposed death. In this liberal use of romance material Sidney was certainly not indifferent to its symbolic resonances, as Shakespeare also understood them in *Pericles*. Man's exposure and vulnerability on the sea of life is an idea relevant to all the shipwrecks of *New Arcadia*, but the second story of treachery and fire at sea, has special significance. Its origin is in human evil and owes nothing to the elements. It derives from the villainy of Plexirtus whose wickedness masquerades in the guise of good, and it works to produce widespread doubt and uncertainty, so that it becomes hard to tell friend from foe, and virtue is hamstrung in its attempts effectively to combat vice. In this confusion, good men as well as bad perish. Plexirtus is the embodiment of the insidious evil that deceives and destroys, and it is totally unlikely that any continuation of his story would have brought him to true repentance.

Offered time and again the chance to repent and redeem himself, Plexirtus uses it only to wade further and further into sin. Cecropia also is offered her chance to repent and does not take it. She, like Plexirtus, is ambitious, ruthless, and potentially, if not actually, murderous. She is not threatened with punishment and then forgiven, as Plexirtus is, but a most conspicuous opportunity to repent her evil ways occurs during the imprisonment of the princesses and especially in the contact she has with Pamela. She rejects it, and death comes to her through her son, whom she has loved, though even love in such a nature is a poison. Cecropia has been shown in unmistakable terms her duty to God, but she will accept neither instruction nor example. Whereas Plexirtus is a wily, scheming, hypocritical villain, she is a strong-willed woman who scorns pretence and pursues her ends openly and singlemindedly. Though they are distinguished in their villainy, their guilt is equal and both condemn themselves by their determination to persist in evil, not through ignorance of alternatives and opportunities to retract but from deliberate choice.

Plexirtus and Cecropia stand together at one extreme on a scale of good and evil. Amphialus and Gynecia also make a pair, this time as twin studies of characters with attributes of highest nobility who succumb to temptation and totter on the brink of joining Plexirtus and Cecropia as figures of evil. The stories of Amphialus and Gynecia have been sufficiently described already, but what is finally to be made of them may still remain a question. Gynecia, in the agony of her guilt and shame when she sees Basilius apparently dead at her feet, passes harsh judgment upon herself. Though she has been entirely ignorant of the effects of the drink and has, in fact, warned Basilius not to take it, her sense of other guilt makes her insist that she is guilty of his murder and she urges Philanax and Euarchus to condemn her. When Basilius rises, as it were from the dead, his first act is to exonerate Gynecia from all blame, "and so with all the exaltings of her that might be, he publicly desired her pardon for those errors he had committed" (OA, 416; P, 847). She does not abuse her pardon, for it is recorded that during the rest of her life she observes "all duty and faith, to the example and glory of Greece." Sidney's final comment on her history is a generalization: "So uncertain are mortal judgements, the same person most infamous, and most famous, and neither justly." This comment is not ironic.[9] Sidney means what he says and what he has been illustrating throughout the trial scene and elsewhere. Mortal judgments *are* uncertain; both virtue and vice can go under false colors, and the best intentioned and the wisest can be deceived. Yet providence, which drives men and women to their limits that they may see and be humbled by their ultimate insufficiency as arbiters of their own fate, works in the end to save the savable. Gynecia is savable because she genuinely repents. Cecropia is not, because even in her dying moments she is "desperate but not repenting" (NA, 440; P, 573).

Amphialus's journey to final redemption is a harder one than even Gynecia's, for the nature of the evil that has to be exorcised is less easy to detect than hers. Her adulterous passion and the excesses it leads her to are always entirely recognizable for what they are, but the trait of character that leads him harshly to repudiate Helen, and then to press his suit to Philoclea, although she begs him to desist, is so mixed in with honorable and noble attributes that it is harder to detect and extirpate. The care and sensitivity given to his choice of clothing and jewels for that first meeting with Philoclea in his castle express real qualities of his nature, but his limp remains and cripples all he does. Amphialus cannot cure himself, but the indications are that he will be healed by love. He might have been a harsh example of Calvinist predestination; instead he is a striking and even intimidating warning of the remorseless progress of a once admitted evil, till its consequences pass out of control. Because, nevertheless, his better nature is never quite subdued, the process of corruption is finally halted and will be reversed.

Individually, Gynecia and Amphialus are imagined with extraordinary subtlety and sympathy. Together, these twin studies of fine but tainted natures constitute a remarkable piece of intellectual discrimination as Sidney traces two distinct kinds of moral history. He works them out to two different kinds of conclusion, but both witness to an order governing human affairs that seeks to regenerate, whenever regeneration is made possible by the cooperation of the individual, however far astray he or she may have gone among the temptations and confusions of this life. The responsibility of the characters for their own state goes together, of course, and paradoxically, with the predetermined nature of the fiction in which they exist, the author's "fore-conceit" as Sidney calls it. Sidney does not in the least attempt to conceal this fact; on the contrary, he draws attention to it by the oracle that forecasts the events that are to occur.[10] The original oracular pronouncement occurring in book 1 of *Old Arcadia* and book 2 of *New* is not prescriptive. Events are forecast but in a way that is open to misinterpretation, and is indeed misinterpreted, and the reactions of those concerned are left unspecified. In every sense, they are free to make what they can of what the future holds. When Basilius sends to Delphos for the second time, however, for advice on how to respond to Anaxius's demand that he and his brothers be allowed to marry the princesses and "Zelmane," he gets a specific answer, couched "not in dark wonted speeches but plainly to be understood" (NA, 457; P, 586), and Philanax is given a special warning that he should not overestimate the capacity of human reason to arrive at true wisdom. In the creation and organization of his fictional world, Sidney enacts a miniature version of the role of the Divine Disposer in the world of men, and the analogy holds at this point. By allowing for both determinism and free will within the story, he reflects the perennial human concern about the nature and limits of each in relation to earthly experience. For him as creator of a world, the stress is on complex and controlled organization; for the characters who people that world, the emphasis is on choice and free will. They are not left entirely without experience of the hand of the creator, however, and when it intervenes, it is an agent of salvation. Even those who ultimately put themselves beyond rescue are given chance after chance to come within the pale of redemption.

The stories of Plexirtus and Cecropia, Gynecia and Amphialus, provide the perspective in which the activities of Pyrocles and Musidorus can properly be seen. They are certainly not wicked, as Plexirtus and Cecropia are; and if they are susceptible to the temptations of passion, like Gynecia and Amphialus, they never wholly succumb or allow their better natures to be corrupted by them. The difference is very marked as all four are brought near to death; Gynecia, expecting imminent execution, is full of self-reproach and horror; Amphialus's last days, before he is carried, half-dead, out of Arcadia, are a sequence of shames and miseries, culminating in the terrible elegy he speaks on himself; Pyrocles and Musidorus, on the other hand, though imprisoned and expecting a death accompanied with disgrace, retain their power to win the love and admiration of good men who come in contact with them and retain also their clear consciences. The account they give of their lives as they prepare for death contrasts absolutely with the summary that Amphialus is driven to give of his:

> "We have lived, and have lived to be good to ourselves and to others. Our souls, which are put into the stirring earth of our bodies, have achieved the causes of their hither coming. They have known and honoured with knowledge the cause of their creation, and to many men (for in this time, place and fortune, it is lawful for us to speak gloriously) it hath been behoveful that we should live." (OA, 371; P, 803)

Sidney exposes his princes to many perils in *New Arcadia*, not only or more importantly of a physical kind, but as he opens out fold after fold of the implications of his action, it becomes increasingly clear that they emerge with credit, fallible human beings certainly, but firmly oriented toward virtue and purged and refined by what they have undergone.

When Pyrocles and Musidorus were very young and before they went out into the world, they were carefully trained for the great positions they would occupy, and even their play was made instructive. Among other things, their "delight of tales" was "converted to the knowledge of all the stories of worthy princes, both to move them to do nobly and teach them how to do nobly" (NA, 163; P, 258). According to the self-reflexive method characteristic of *New Arcadia*, they themselves become a story of worthy princes, in the course of it both learning and teaching how to do nobly. Such a story is less effective, "moves" less, if it contains no possibility of wrongdoing, but, equally, it can admit of no serious failures. Musidorus, more mature at the end of the book than he was at the beginning, addresses some cogent remarks to Euarchus in his capacity as judge and, in defense of himself and Pyrocles claims that "our doing in the extremist interpretation is but human error" (OA, 402; P, 833). The "errors" committed by the princes are more serious in *Old Arcadia* than in *New*, and when he revised his book, Sidney modified the lovemaking episodes and, more importantly, developed the stories of Cecropia, Plexirtus, Gynecia, and Amphialus to clarify what he understood as the real nature of sin and the reach of divine forgiveness. The moral standing of the princes is, as a result, put beyond doubt, and judgment such as Euarchus passes comes to reflect mostly on the limitations of human reason. In this it is fully consistent with a theme that the revision emphasizes, as also is Basilius's resuscitation to pronounce forgiveness to all who have in one degree or another erred but not committed themselves beyond recall to evil. *Arcadia*, in both its forms, is a humane work. *New Arcadia* especially is clear-sighted but generous, probing but sympathetic. "The web of our life is of a mingled yarn, good and ill together: our virtues would be proud if our faults whipped them not; and our crimes would despair if they were not cherished by our virtues." So says an unnamed lord in Shakespeare's *All's Well that Ends Well*. The words could serve as an epigraph for *Arcadia*, though Sidney, no doubt, would have wished to add that virtue itself needs to be sustained by a divine hand.

Notes

Preface

1. William Archer, *The Old Drama and the New* (London, Cambridge, Mass: Heinemann, 1923).
2. See *The Penguin Book of Elizabethan Verse*, ed. Edward Lucie-Smith (Harmondsworth: Penguin, 1965), and *Ten Elizabethan Poets*, ed. Philip Hobsbaum (London: Longmans, 1969).
3. Brian Vickers in *The Times Literary Supplement*, November 18–24. II. 1988.
4. T. S. Eliot, *The Use of Poetry and the Use of Criticism* (London: Faber, 1933).
5. Jean Robertson, ed., *The Countess of Pembroke's "Arcadia": the Old Arcadia* (Oxford: Clarendon Press, 1973); Victor Skretkowicz, ed., *The New Arcadia*, (Oxford: Clarendon Press, 1987).
6. J. O'Connor, *"Amadis de Gaule" and Its Influence on Elizabethan Literature* (New Brunswick, N.J.: Rutgers University Press, 1970).
7. A. C. Hamilton, "Sidney's *Arcadia* as Prose Fiction: Its Relation to Its Sources," *English Literary Renaissance* 2 (1972): 29–60.
8. "Divided Aims in the *Revised Arcadia*," in *Sir Philip Sidney and the Interpretation of Renaissance Culture*, ed. Gary F. Waller and Michael D. Moore (London and Sydney: Croom Helm; Totowa, N.J.: Barnes and Noble Books, 1984).
9. C. S. Lewis, *English Literature in the Sixteenth Century* (Oxford: Clarendon Press, 1954).
10. *Sir Philip Sidney and the Interpretation of Renaissance Culture;* Jan Van Dorsten, Dominic Baker-Smith, and Arthur F. Kinney, eds., *Sir Philip Sidney: 1586 and the Creation of a Legend* (Leiden: Sir Thomas Browne Institute, 1986); ed. Dennis Kay, *Sir Philip Sidney: An Anthology of Modern Criticism* (Oxford: Clarendon Press, 1987). See my reviews in *Cahiers Elisabéthains*, October 1986 and October 1989.
11. Nancy Lindheim, *The Structures of Sidney's Arcadia* (Toronto, London: University of Toronto Press, 1982).
12. John Carey, "Structure and Rhetoric in Sidney's *Arcadia*," in *Sir Philip Sidney: An Anthology of Modern Criticism*, ed. Kay.

Introduction

1. Steuart A. Pears, ed., *The Correspondence of Sir Philip Sidney and Hubert Languet*, (London, 1845), 143.
2. John Gouws, ed., *The Prose Works of Fulke Greville, Lord Brooke* (Oxford: Clarendon Press, 1986), 77.
3. See L. Stone, *The Crisis of the Aristocracy, 1558–1641* (Oxford University Press, 1967), 18. Stone is less than fair to Lord Herbert, for he neglects to mention the sending of other boats. For Herbert's own account, see J. M. Shuttleworth, ed., *The Life of Lord Herbert of Cherbury*, (London, New York, Toronto: Oxford University Press, 1976), 50–52.

4. Geoffrey Shepherd, ed., *An Apology for Poetry*, (London: Nelson's Medieval and Renaissance Library, 1965), 104.

5. James M. Osborn, *Young Philip Sidney* (New Haven and London: Yale University Press, 1972), 513.

6. Ibid., 513–14.

7. John Buxton, *Sir Philip Sidney and the English Renaissance* (London: Macmillan; New York: St Martin's Press, 1964), 112.

8. Public Record Office SP12 / 195 / 33. The text of the letter is given in *The Poems of Sir Philip Sidney*, ed. W. A. Ringler (Oxford: Clarendon Press, 1962), p. 530; and in Joan Rees, *Fulke Greville, Lord Brooke* (London: Routledge & Kegan Paul, 1971), 46–47.

9. Jean Robertson, ed., *The Countess of Pembroke's Arcadia (The Old Arcadia)*, xxxvii.

10. See *An Apology for Poetry*, ed. Shepherd, where Sidney writes: "Truly, I have known men, that even with reading *Amadis de Gaule* (which God knoweth wanteth much of a perfect poesy) have found their hearts moved to the exercise of courtesy, liberality, and especially courage" (114). John O'Connor, in his book *"Amadis de Gaule" and Its Influence on Elizabethan Literature*, comments that in the Amadisian code "sexual gratification is almost a knight's prerogative and a lady's constancy is much more important than her chastity" (196).

Chapter 1. Heroes and Heroics

1. A limp as a moral emblem is also used by Petrarch in *Rime* 88 and 214 and perhaps by Shakespeare in Sonnet 89.

2. John Danby, *Elizabethan and Jacobean Poets* (London: Faber and Faber, 1965) 73.

3. See Martin Bergbusch, "Rebellion in the *New Arcadia*" *Philological Quarterly* 53 (1974): 29–41 for a full discussion of this.

4. Cf. Hamilton, "Sidney's *Arcadia* as Prose Fiction," 29–60, where he writes that Argalus and Parthenia "provide the pattern of constant affection which measures all the lovers, and their marriage is the ideal state which all should seek."

5. It may be relevant to recall the Diana-Actaeon myth in relation to the scene of Amphialus's first sight of Philoclea. W. R. Davis in "Actaeon in *Arcadia*," *Studies in English Literature, 1500–1900* 2 (1962): 95–110, has an interesting discussion of the myth in reference to the meeting in a cave of Pyrocles and Gynecia, which takes place in *Old Arcadia*. The Amphialus-Philoclea scene is a more direct parallel. Amphialus is accompanied by a dog, which enforces the likeness, but Amphialus's dog is an attractive little creature. This seems to be a characteristically Sidneyan way, recognized in retrospect, of foretelling that Amphialus will not ultimately share the fate of Acteon. The myth tells that he was torn to pieces by his own hounds, a story usually moralized as meaning that ungoverned passion destroyed him. Amphialus, however, is saved.

6. See the discussion of Amphialus as a "surrogate hero" in Lindheim, *The Structures of Sidney's Arcadia*, 81–86. Lindheim sees the importance of Amphialus to Pyrocles and Musidorus but attributes the disasters of his career to the need to compensate for the primary heroes' "good luck." My argument is that the moral underpinning of the distinctions between Amphialus and Pyrocles and Musidorus goes a good deal deeper than that. McCoy's comments (*Sir Philip Sidney: Rebellion in Arcadia* (Brighton: Harvester Press, 1979) that "the pathos of futile courtship becomes his [Amphialus's] definitive characteristic" and that he is treated by Sidney

with "indulgent admiration" (188, 189) seem to me entirely mistaken.

In "Architectonic Knowledge in the *New Arcadia* (1590): Sidney's Use of the Heroic Journey," *Salzburg Studies in English Literature* 69 (1978), Josephine A. Roberts considers in general terms Amphialus's relation to other characters. She finds him lacking in "architectonic knowledge" (Sidney's phrase in the *Apology*, ed. Shepherd, 104). She writes that "He believes in the model of the self-centered warrior and does not recognize that the heroic life may consist of higher values" (246). Again, my argument is that Sidney's conception of the character of Amphialus and its function in *New Arcadia* goes well beyond any such description.

7. See also OA, 52, when he kisses Pamela "a hundred times" as she swoons after the bear's attack. This was all changed in the *New Arcadia* version of the scene (NA, 115; P, 179–80).

8. Shakespeare's conception of Cloten in *Cymbeline* may owe something to Sidney's handling of Amphialus for, like Amphialus (though, of course, incomparably meaner of nature), Cloten has something of the role of a surrogate. His function is not merely that of the worthless bully, for at one point Posthumus is actually identified with him when Imogen grieves over the headless body, believing it to be that of her husband. Posthumus himself can be foul-mouthed and vicious, and he has to be purged of his likeness to Cloten just as Pyrocles and Musidorus have to be detached from the weaknesses they share with Amphialus. *Cymbeline*, in fact, as the first fully worked out example of the late romance pattern in the Shakespeare canon, shows several Sidneyan features: a deluded king is enlightened and pronounces "Pardon's the word for all," and the quality of lovers and princes is established by contrasts. Leo Salingar writes of the "Chinese-box technique of disclosing successive identities in a judicial hearing," which Shakespeare had used in *The Comedy of Errors (Shakespeare and the Tradition of Comedy* London: Cambridge University Press, 1974), and comments that he was to stretch it "to the limits of ingenuity" at the end of *Cymbeline* (29). Disclosure of successive identities in a judicial hearing is, of course, what happens at the end of *Arcadia* where Euarchus, Pyrocles, and Musidorus are found to be father, son, and nephew and Basilius is revealed, in a great *coup de théâtre*, to be not a dead corpse but a living man, able to fulfill his role as ruler and make possible the fulfillment of love.

Chapter 2. Stella and the Growth of the Heroine

1. J. H. Whitfield, *A Short History of Italian Literature* (Harmondsworth: Penguin, 1960), 28.

2. A. J. Smith, *The Metaphysics of Love*, (Cambridge: Cambridge University Press, 1985).

3. Castiglione, *The Book of the Courtier*, trans. Sir Thomas Hoby (London: Dent, 1974), 324.

4. As Du Bellay's Olive has been described by A. L. Prescott, *French Poets and the English Renaissance* (New Haven, Conn.; London: Yale University Press, 1978), 38.

5. George Watson, *The English Petrarchans*, (London: *Warburg Institute Surveys*, no. 3, 1967).

6. Castiglione, *The Book of the Courtier,* 315.

Chapter 3. Sidney and the Characters of Women

1. Lewis, *English Literature in the Sixteenth Century*, 338.

2. Danby, *Elizabethan and Jacobean Poets*, 58.

3. Greville, *Prose Works*, 10.

4. Except curiously, at a point in the new book 3 when Pyrocles, the defender of women in the early argument, becomes briefly but unrestrainedly abusive (NA, 434; P, 566–69). He has the excuse that he believes both Pamela and Philoclea to be dead, at the hands of Cecropia, and he is nearly out of his mind with grief and his own inability to have assisted them. Sidney, with his quizzical sense of the ironies in human behavior, seems to be registering his observation that abuse of women comes readily to the tongues of even generous and sympathetic men when caught off balance and looking for someone to blame for discomfort or disaster.

5. S. L. Wolff, *The Greek Romances in Elizabethan Prose Fiction*, (New York: Columbia University Studies in Comparative Literature, 1912), says that Sidney derived Gynecia from Achilles Tatius but, if this is so, Sidney's originality is all the more striking. In Tatius's treatment of the strong-minded and passionate Melissa there is none of the psychological analysis and moral balancing that Sidney employs in his treatment of Gynecia. It is true that Tatius is not without sympathy for Melissa's love, but he allows her both to enjoy Theagenes and to escape scot-free, and this Sidney did not and would not, conceivably, have done.

The same point holds true for whatever hint of an idea for Gynecia Sidney derived from *Amadis de Gaule*. Sidney gives extra dimensions to the *Amadis* characters, which totally transform their role and function. Cf. Jean Robertson (OA, xxiv): "In spite of the moral benefits that Sidney claimed could be derived from reading *Amadis de Gaule*, neither it nor the Greek romances had any real ethos behind the sentiment and the emotion."

6. The letter episode derives ultimately from Montemayor's *Diana*, as does the similar scene in *Two Gentlemen of Verona*, act 1, scene 2.

7. The comparable passage in *Old Arcadia* (OA, 108–9) is much shorter, and has some substantial differences.

8. In the end Pamphilus marries "the most impudently unchaste woman of all Asia" (NA, 260; P, 358), an example of the sharp eye Sidney keeps on all the details of his canvas.

9. In *Old Arcadia* (OA, 39) Pyrocles's special attention to Philoclea when he is first received into the royal company causes, Sidney suggests, "some little envy in the other ladies, to see young Philoclea's beauty so greatly advanced." In *New Arcadia* this slight but unworthy slur is removed.

10. See, for example, Mark Rose, "Sidney's Womanish Man," *Review of English Studies*, n.s. 15, 1964, 353–63.

11. The princess Pamela, as Pyrocles describes her, wears a shepherd's dress and with it a rich jewel inscribed "Yet still myself." The motto is a paradox. She, like Pyrocles, is in a dress that belies her true state, but her motto affirms that her nature is essentially unchanged. Sidney introduced both her and Pyrocles' mottoes into *New Arcadia* (compare NA, 84 and 69; P, 146 and 131; with OA, 37 and 27) and evidently intended a point to be taken. That the mottoes state the literal truth, as well for Pyrocles as for Pamela, may be confirmed by other references in *New Arcadia:* of Argalus, "no man for valour of mind and ability of body to be preferred, if equalled, to Argalus; and yet so valiant as he never durst do anybody injury" (NA, 27; P, 87); and Pyrocles' love is said to be "valiant" because it accepts restraint (NA, 234; P, 331).

12. Maurice Evans makes an extraordinarily impercipient comment on this scene in the course of an article that is generally unsympathetic to the text he has edited. "By the end of Book 3," he writes "he [Sidney] is driven for the sake of variety to the verge of 'camp' in the long unfinished fight between Anaxius and Pyrocles in woman's dress. Perhaps the very flippancy of what he found himself doing was a

reason why he stopped" ("Divided Aims in the Revised *Arcadia*," in *Sir Philip Sidney and the Interpretation of Renaissance Culture* ed. Waller and Moore, pp. 34–43. Sidney's treatment of Pyrocles' female disguise produces other curious comments, such as that of David Norbrook who writes: "Basilius' retreat is a sign of effeminacy, a fact symbolised by his falling in love with Pyrocles in his female disguise" *Poetry and Politics in the English Renaissance* (London: Routledge and Kegan Paul. 1984, 95).

13. Thelma N. Greenfield, in *The Eye of Judgment* (London: Associated University Presses, 1982), brings together evidence from life, iconography, and literature, and from Plato and Jung, to counter the idea that Pyrocles' disguise must necessarily be thought of by Sidney and others as humiliating. She remarks, justly, that the "transformed hero performs greatly within his disguise" (62) and comments: "To that part of the age which preserved its faith in iconography, symbolic 'transvestism' would be a glorious transcendence rather than a reductive perversion" (60). John Danby made a similar point when he wrote (*Elizabethan and Jacobean Poets*, 57) that Pyrocles' female dress "adds to rather than diminishes his merely masculine virtue."

14. Greville, *Prose Works*, 4–5. The story of Parthenia's disfigurement seems to recall this episode of family life and may have been intended as a tribute to the conduct of Sidney's mother and father at this time.

15. Ibid., 133.

16. So far the only complete edition of Daniel's work is that of the Rev. A. B. Grosart, 5 vols. (London: Hazell, Watson & Viney, 1885–96).

17. Daniel was a member of the Countess of Pembroke's household at Wilton for some years beginning in 1591–92. He is very likely to have read a manuscript of *Old Arcadia* at that time. See, for his connection with Sidney and the Pembrokes, Joan Rees, *Samuel Daniel: A Critical and Biographical Study* (Liverpool: Liverpool University Press, 1964).

Chapter 4. Telling the Tales

1. See Myron Turner's generally interesting article "The Disfigured Face of Nature," *English Literary Renaissance* 2 (1972): 116–35, for a comment on the monster. He writes that "the slaying of the monster Tyranny (so Spenser might have called it)" is part of "the symbolic value of Pyrocles' final quest in Asia" (129–30).

2. Thelma Greenfield in *The Eye of Judgment* thinks it is a "letdown" when the practical use of the sword is disclosed, but she adds that the revelation illustrates "Sidney's care in tying up the tiniest string with logical cause" (89).

3. Katherine Duncan-Jones, "Sidney's Urania," *Review of English Studies* n.s. 17 (1966): 123–32.

4. Ringler, *Poems*, 403–4.

5. There are two other passages referring to Urania in *New Arcadia* (NA, 97 and 99–100, P, 160 and 162–63). They function principally, as they stand, to make a contrast between a lowly shepherd and shepherdess and the high-born persons by whom they are surrounded. The contrast is entirely in favor of the humble, but without the completion of *New Arcadia* the relation of these passages to the book as a whole remains obscure. Most studies of *New Arcadia* speculate on the nature and role of Urania. For discussion in a wider context, see Alan Sinfield, "Sidney and DuBartas," *Comparative Literature* 27 (Winter 1975): 8–20.

6. On the great mass of "friendship literature," see the Arden edition of *Two Gentlemen of Verona*, ed. Clifford Leach, Introduction, Section 3, Sources.

7. Duncan-Jones, "Sidney's Urania."

8. Sidney even gives to Philoclea a version of David's lament for Jonathan: "Pamela, my sister! my sister Pamela! Woe is me for thee! I would I had died for thee!" (NA, 426; P, 558)

9. Lorna Challis discusses the topic in "The Use of Oratory in Sidney's *Arcadia*," *Journal of English and Germanic Philology* 62 (1965): 561–76.

10. Bacon's essay "Of Travel" sets out the proper procedure.

11. R. S. White in "Metamorphosis by Love in Elizabethan Romance, Romantic Comedy, and Shakespeare's Early Comedies," *Review of English Studies* 35 (1984): 14–44, is among those who think that Musidorus is expressing Sidney's own view. This could be so only if Sidney were a conventional thinker, content to reiterate received platitudes. This he is not. In so far as the old debate of reason versus passion underlies much of the activity of *Arcadia*, it is not to be assumed that Sidney sees the issues as clear-cut. Nancy Lindheim concludes her analysis of the antithetical topoi she finds in *New Arcadia* by pointing to "the tension between Sidney's analytic mode of thought (which sees the world in terms of antithetical alternatives) and the harmonious, synthetic nature of his vision of the ideal" (410). See also Dorothy Connell's discussion of *Arcadia* in her book *Sir Philip Sidney: The Maker's Mind* (Oxford: Clarendon Press, 1977). She ascribes to Sidney a quality that she accepts as characteristic of Renaissance thought, i.e., "an ability to encompass and balance contradictions" (4–5). To believe that he shares Musidorus's position here is not only to ignore the range and depth of his explorations in *Arcadia* but also to be deaf to the tone of this scene with its glancing ironies and lightness of touch.

Rosalie L. Colie has some relevant remarks in "The Rhetoric of Transcendence," *Philological Quarterly* 43 (1964): 145–70: "Erasmus, Montaigne, and Hamlet, together with the host of Stoic writers concerned with knowing themselves, were engaged in something other than the moral self-examination required by religious tradition and exemplified in manuals of devotional meditation, but in something more cutting, the self-conscious effort to understand understanding, their own and that of mankind." Of a group of poems, including Fulke Greville's "Treatie of Humane Learning," Colie writes: "These strongly Christian poems are all in the stoical tradition and owe a debt to their sceptical inheritance; their poets were engaged in fulfilling their Christian-humanist obligation to know themselves, and to know how they knew what they knew." This is a climate familiar to Sidney. Musidorus in the debate belongs to an old school: Pyrocles is responding (anachronistically) to the newer influences of Sidney's day.

12. Sidney, *An Apology for Poetry*, ed. Shepherd, 139.

13. Jonas Barish, "The Prose Style of John Lyly," *English Literary History:* 22–23 (1956): 14–35.

14. R. W. Bond, ed., *Complete Works of John Lyly*, (Oxford: Clarendon Press, 1902), 1: 80.

15. P. Albert Duhamel, "Sidney's *Arcadia* and Elizabethan Rhetoric," *Studies in Philology* 45, Vol. 1 (1948): 134–50. In "John Lyly and Elizabethan Rhetoric," *Studies in Philology* 52 (1955): 149–61, W. N. King takes issue with Duhamel and argues that his analysis of Lyly fails to take account of some dramatic qualities in Lyly's prose. He claims that Lyly adapts the rhetorical set piece in *Euphues* for purposes of narrative and characterization. He makes his points well, but they cannot be stretched far to modify what has been said above in comparing Lyly with Sidney.

16. Maurice Evans's introduction to the Penguin *Arcadia* gives a sympathetic account of Sidney's rhetoric (14–19). There are also some good and appreciative comments in the chapter "Focus and Style" in Thelma N. Greenfield's *The Eye of Judgment*.

17. This passage does not occur in the Old *Arcadia* version of the scene—evidence (though the fact is self-evident) of Sidney's deliberate interest in the theory and practice of narrative in his rewriting of *Arcadia*.

18. Clinias's speech is given in exactly the same words in *Old Arcadia* (OA, 131) but there it stands as a somewhat sententious authorial comment. The change is a very interesting detail of revision, showing at the same time Sidney's developed interest in dramatic qualities and in character, and the sophisticated understanding of political behavior he is now feeding into his fiction.

19. Clinias was evidently trained in the same school of acting as that with which Richard of Gloucester and the Duke of Buckingham are familiar in Shakespeare's *Richard III*—see the beginning of act 3.

20. For the influence of Heliodorus on *New Arcadia*, see Wolff's *The Greek Romances in Elizabethan Prose Fiction*. The romances of Heliodorus, Longus, and Achilles Tatius are translated by Rowland Smith in *The Greek Romances* (London: Bohun's Libraries, 1901). Sidney makes several commendatory references to Heliodorus's "sugared invention of that picture of love in Theagenes and Chariclea" in his *Apology for Poetry*. See also V. Skretkowicz, "Sidney and Amyot: Heliodorus in *New Arcadia*," *Review of English Studies* (1976): 170–74.

21. V. O. Freeburg in *Disguise Plots in Elizabethan Drama*, (New York: Columbia University Studies in English and Comparative Literature, 1915), gives useful summaries of disguise plots.

22. See R. H. Perkinson, "The Epic in Five Acts," *Studies in Philology* 43 (1946): 465–81; and R. W. Parker, "Terentian Structure in Sidney's Original *Arcadia*," *English Literary Renaissance* 2 (1972): 61–78.

23. The uncertainties and confusions that develop increasingly in New Arcadia have been noticed before and are usually interpreted in relatively straightforward moralistic terms. Nancy R. Lindheim, for instance, in an interesting article, "Sidney's *Arcadia* Book II: Retrospective Narrative," *Studies in Philology* 64 (1967): 159–86, suggests that "the confusions arise from the conflict between order and chaos"; but such explanations do not do justice to either the art or the morality of *New Arcadia*.

24. In this it is strikingly different from Spenser's *Faerie Queene*, a work with which *Arcadia* is often, though misleadingly, compared. There are no internal debates in *The Faerie Queene*, no situations in which a good character may be genuinely at a loss as to how to comport him- or herself (although he or she may be led astray) and no situation in which a bad character is modified by some touch of humanity. Sidney, on the other hand, involves the reader in the intimate experience of complex characters faced with ambiguous situations. Yet the assurances that are missing from the lives lived in *New Arcadia* are present in the author's design and organization of the whole, whereas Spenser's moral judgments stand within a structure that notably lacks the precise engineering of Sidney's. Many attempts to identify the organizational principle of *The Faerie Queene* bear witness to this. The result is that, although the care of heaven for the Christian wayfarer is stressed on many occasions and the Mutabilitie Cantos make their claim for ultimate order, the security of Sidney's authorial providence, reflecting the assurance of God's plan for the world, is not to be found in the poem.

25. Sidney's word was "wormish," a different sentiment entirely.

26. There is a similar play between the writer and one of his characters in the scene where Musidorus, as the shepherd Dorus, begins to tell Pamela his own history under the guise of reporting somebody else's. Pamela has questioned part of the story and Musidorus replies: "I perceive indeed you have neither heard or read the story of that unhappy prince [Musidorus]; for this was the very objection which the peerless

princess did make unto him when he sought to appear such as he was before her wisdom: and thus, as I have read it fair written, in the certainty of my knowledge he might answer her" (NA, 137; P, 231). A character who depends for his existence on writing and reading claims to have read what his creator is at that moment composing. The character is himself fictionalizing for he knows that nothing has been written and that Musidorus's answer comes into being only at the moment that he, Musidorus, makes it. The relation of life to literature and of the author to his characters and of fictional time to "real" time are all involved in this witty passage.

27. In "Differences of Theme and Structure of the Erona Episode in the *Old* and *New Arcadia*," *Studies in Philology* 70 (1973): 377–91, Winifred Schleiner exaggerates the importance of Antiphilus's low birth: his humble origin is only one of many elements in this most carefully worked story. The accounts by Lindheim and W. R. Davis (*A Map of Arcadia*, New Haven and London: Yale University Press, 1965) are concerned to relate the episode to other retrospective narratives in book 2 rather than to study it in detail for itself.

28. The story of the Paphlagonian king and his two sons, one a bastard and treacherous and the other legitimate, loyal, and devoted, is well known because of Shakespeare's use of it in *King Lear*. Its ramifications in *New Arcadia* are very extensive, the bastard son being Plexirtus, whose evil is allowed, by the generous treatment accorded him by his brother, to spread over wide areas of the book. For a discussion of Leonatus's leniency to Plexirtus and its implications in *New Arcadia*, see my article, "Justice, Mercy and a Shipwreck in *Arcadia*," *Studies in Philology*, Vol. 87, No. 1 (Winter 1990), 75–82.

29. Andromana's tactics, praising Plangus in such a way as to arouse suspicion of his intentions, are very similar to those used in Fulke Greville's play, *Mustapha*, to convince Soliman that his son means to murder and supplant him. Sidney's and Greville's demonstrations of how effectively this subtle means of undermining an enemy or rival can be used prompts speculation about some common source, perhaps in experience.

30. The episode is modeled on one in Heliodorus's *Ethiopica* (see Wolff, *Greek Romances*, 115–16), and there is a similar episode in *The Revenger's Tragedy*, act 2, scene 3.

31. Those who would make Sidney a severe judge of human conduct should note the narrator's comment on Plangus's behavior. There are certainly "errors in his nature"—which he will have to pay for—but excuse is allowed on grounds of "the greenness of his youth" (NA, 215; P, 312). Philanax is ready to make the same excuse for Amphialus's behavior: "Your fault past is excusable, in that love persuaded and youth was persuaded" (NA, 353; P, 482).

32. Greville, *Prose Works*, 12.

33. It is a notable point of Sidney's tact (and common sense) in handling Pyrocles' disguise as a woman that Cecropia sees him only once, by torchlight and when her attention is elsewhere (NA, 317; P, 444). Of those who are allowed to get close to Pyrocles as Amazon, only the inexperienced or the foolish are taken in by his disguise and Cecropia would certainly have seen through it.

34. Chapter 3 of W. R. Elton's *"King Lear" and the Gods* (San Marino, California: Huntington Library Publication, 1966) deals in detail with the background of the Pamela/Cecropia argument and provides the necessary references.

35. Sidney does not, in any mood, speak of literature in the terms that Fulke Greville and Milton apply to it. In *Caelica* 66 Greville concludes an attack on books with a last dismissive stanza:

> What then need half-fast helps of erring wit,
> Methods, or books of vain humanity?
> Which dazzle truth, by representing it,
> And so entail clouds to posterity. . . ,

Milton's Christ in *Paradise Regained* is similarly contemptuous of the usefulness of books. Neither Greville nor Milton was thinking of fiction when they made these strictures, for it was beneath the level of serious consideration. Greville made a partial exception for *Arcadia*, though he was uneasy with it; Milton made none. In a passage from *Eikonoklastes*, he categorizes *Arcadia* as "no serious Book." In its kind he allows that it is "full of worth and witt," but among religious thoughts and duties not worthy to be nam'd; nor to be read at any time without good caution." Those who wish to argue that Sidney was himself of a severe Calvinist cast of thought should remember that on this matter of the value of imaginative literature, as on others, Sidney shows a much more liberal attitude.

36. Sidney, *An Apology for Poetry*, ed. Shepherd, 133.

37. Cf. W. R. Davis, "Thematic Unity in *New Arcadia*," *Studies in Philology* 57 (1960): 123–43: "Book II, with the different styles of narrative in the two groups of episodes and the explicit parody of old romance, is in part a treatise on styles in fiction."

Chapter 5. New and Old

1. McCoy, *Rebellion in Arcadia*, 136.

2. See, for example, Jon S. Lawry, *Sidney's Two "Arcadias"* (Ithaca, NY; London: Cornell University Press, 1972) and Andrew D. Weiner, *Sir Philip Sidney and the Poetics of Protestantism* (Minneapolis: University of Minnesota, 1978). The argument was first proposed by Franco Marenco in *Arcadia Puritana* (Bari: Adriatica Editrice, 1968). See also Marenco's "Double Plot in Sidney's *Old Arcadia*" *Modern Language Review* 64 (1969): 248–63, and "Une Apothéose de genres: Sidney e l'Arcadia nella critica letteraria," *Filologia e Letteratura* 4 (1966): 337–76.

3. This suggestion, made by Ringler, 383, is endorsed by Jean Robertson, lxii.

4. Sidney, *Poems*, ed. Ringler, 260–64.

5. Greville, *Prose Works*, 134.

6. See Joan Rees, *Fulke Greville, Lord Brooke*, 90–103.

7. The latest editor, John Gouws, prefers to entitle it *A Dedication to Sir Philip Sidney*. It is doubtful whether the change is worth making.

8. Greville, *Prose Works*, 12.

9. Ibid., 134.

10. Ibid.

11. Ibid., 11.

12. Ibid., 21.

13. Ibid., 11.

14. For example, Alan Sinfield, "Astrophil's Self-Deception," *Essays in Criticism* 28 (1978): 1–18.

15. *The Correspondence of Sir Philip Sidney and Hubert Languet*, ed. Pears; also, with a different wording, Osborn, *Young Philip Sidney*, 227. Compare with Languet's words two sayings reported of Sidney, one by Ludowick Bryskett: "Say to thy selfe with that worthy bright light of our age Sir Philip Sidney, Let us love men for the good is in them, and not hate them for their evil"; and one by Thomas Gainsford: "as noble

Sir Philip Sidney was wont to say, Let us love him for one good qualitie; for a great many have none at all and no man hath all."

16. Even sympathetic critics of *Arcadia* forget Sidney's humor. Robert W. Parker in "Terentian Structure in Sidney's original *Arcadia*," feels (rightly) that the point needs to be made, if only in a footnote: "I would like to make perfectly clear that I find this a very funny book." He adds, "The combination of sly humour with the serious should surprise no student of Sidney or of the Renaissance."

Chapter 6. Trial and Human Error

1. Sidney, *Apology of Poetry*, ed. Shepherd, 106.
2. D. M. Anderson, in "The Trial of the Princes in *Arcadia* Book V," *Review of English Studies* 8 (1957): 409–12, argues that "The sole preoccupation of Philanax and Euarchus is to punish those who have subverted the order of society and to get the constitution working again." It is not the *sole* preoccupation of Philanax, but Anderson's comment is largely true of Euarchus.
3. Euarchus is in violation of the principle of Equity. Renaissance thinking distinguished between Justice, which was the strict meting out of reward and punishment according to the letter of the law, and Equity, which took account of individual conditions and circumstances. Samuel Daniel's verse epistle to Sir Thomas Egerton makes much of this distinction. In defense of Euarchus's refusal to reconsider his verdict when he knows the truth about the background and careers of the princes, it has to be remembered that Arcadian law, which he has bound himself to administer, explicitly forbids second thoughts: only the King has authority to override this restriction and ensure that, in spite of the law, the right conclusion is arrived at. See also, on the conduct of the trial, Elizabeth Dipple, "Unjust Justice in the *Old Arcadia*," *Studies in English Literature* 10 (1970): 83–101; and, on Euarchus, Margaret E. Dana, "The Providential Plot in the *Old Arcadia*" *Studies in English Literature* 17, (1977) 39–57. Dana writes of "the flexible narrator . . . whose mellow tact and ironic compassion for all the characters finally seem the most humane response to life's riddling text." There is a valuable discussion of what is involved in Euarchus's judgment in A. F. Kinney, "Sidney's Journey to Flushing and Zutphen" in *Sir Philip Sidney: 1586 and the Creation of a Legend*.
4. Greville, *Prose Works*, 81–82.
5. For a discussion of these matters, see D. P. Walker, "Ways of Dealing with Atheists: A Background to Pamela's Refutation of Cecropia," *Bibliothèque d'Humanisme et Renaissance* 17 (1955): 252–77, reprinted as chapter 4 of *Ancient Theology* by the same author (London: Duckworth, 1972), and chapter 3 of Elton's *"King Lear" and the Gods*. Alan Sinfield disagrees with Walker and Elton in "Sidney, Du Plessis Mornay and the Pagans," *Philological Quarterly* (1979): 26–39, but his argument is not convincing.
6. For the background of Pyrocles' and Musidorus's discussion, see OA, 479–80.
7. Dorothy Connell draws attention to changes in this passage in order to stress the revision's deliberate subordination of "human wisdom" to "divine providence" (*Sir Philip Sidney: The Maker's Mind*, 143–45).
8. In *"King Lear" and the Gods*, (63), Elton describes Cecropia as an "inward" atheist, but this is an error for she is very explicit about her amoral, irreligious views. He does not mention Plexirtus.
9. Still less is it "a typically caustic remark" (editor's comment, P, 879). To read it like this is to be insensitive to the whole ethos of *Arcadia* and to Sidney himself

whose wit is pointed, but not designed to sear. Cf. Spenser's second thoughts when, reporting to Gabriel Harvey that Gosson was scorned by Sidney for dedicating *The School of Abuse* to him, he adds "if at leaste it be in the goodnesse of that nature to scorne" (*Poetical Works*, ed. E. de Selincourt (London, Oxford University Press, 1929), 635.

10. A point that deserves to be noted is a small change made in the 1593 account of Euarchus's arrival in Arcadia. In *Old Arcadia*, among his motives for visiting Basilius, is an intention to arrange for the marriages of his son and nephew with the Arcadian princesses. In the 1593 version this consideration is omitted and there is no mention of projected marriages. Sidney evidently intended, on revision, that the exertions and trials of the princes in the course of their wooing should have full value as educative experience and should not be depreciated by the discovery that they could have won their brides without any trouble if only they had been content to let events take their course. The effect is to emphasize individual responsibility and reduce the influence of the predetermined. On the function of the oracle in *Arcadia*, see Michael McCanles, "Oracular Prediction and the Foreconceit of Sidney's *Arcadia*," *English Literary History* 50, no. 2 (1983): 233–44.

Select Bibliography

Sidney's Works

An Apology for Poetry. Edited by Geoffrey Shepherd. London and Edinburgh: Nelson, 1965.

The Correspondence of Sir Philip Sidney and Hubert Languet. Edited by Steuart A. Pears. London, 1845.

The Countess of Pembroke's Arcadia (The Old Arcadia). Edited by Jean Robertson. Oxford: Clarendon Press, 1973.

Arcadia. Edited by Maurice Evans. Harmondsworth: Penguin, 1977.

The Countess of Pembroke's Arcadia (The New Arcadia). Edited by Victor Skretkowicz. Oxford: Clarendon Press, 1987.

The Poems of Sir Philip Sidney. Edited by W. A. Ringler. Oxford: Clarendon Press, 1962.

Other Works

Anderson, D. M. "The Trial of the Princes in the *Arcadia* Book V." *Review of English Studies* 8 (1957): 409–12.

Archer, William. *The Old Drama and the New.* London and Cambridge, Mass.: Heinemann, 1923.

Bacon, Francis. *Essays.*

Barish, Jonas A., "The Prose Style of John Lyly." *English Literary History* 22–23 (1956): 14–35.

Bergbusch, Martin, "Rebellion in the *New Arcadia.*" *Philological Quarterly* 53 (1974): 29–41.

Buxton, John. *Sir Philip Sidney and the English Renaissance.* London: Macmillan; New York: St. Martin's Press, 1964.

Carey, John. "Structure and Rhetoric in Sidney's *Arcadia.*" In *Sir Philip Sidney: An Anthology of Modern Criticism,* edited by Dennis Kay.

Castiglione, B. *The Book of the Courtier.* Transl. by Sir Thomas Hoby. London: Dent, 1974.

Challis, Lorna, "The Use of Oratory in Sidney's *Arcadia.*" *Journal of English and Germanic Philology* 62 (1965): 561–76.

Colie, Rosalie L., "The Rhetoric of Transcendence." *Philological Quarterly* 43 (1964): 145–70.

Connell, Dorothy. *Sir Philip Sidney: The Maker's Mind.* Oxford: Clarendon Press, 1977.

Dana, M. E. "The Providential Plot of the Old Arcadia." *Studies in English Literature* 17 (1977): 39–57.

Danby, John F. *Elizabethan and Jacobean Poets.* London: Faber, 1965.

Daniel, Samuel. *Complete Works in Verse and Prose.* Edited by A. B. Grosart. London: Hazel, Watson and Viney, 1885–96. 5 vols.

Davis, W. R. "Thematic Unity in the *New Arcadia.*" *Studies in Philology* 57 (1960): 123–43.

———. "Actaeon in Arcadia." *Studies in English Literature* 2(1962): 95–110.

———. *A Map of Arcadia.* New Haven and London: Yale University Press, 1965.

Dipple, Elizabeth, "Unjust Justice in the *Old Arcadia.*" *Studies in English Literature* 10 (1970): 83–101.

Dorsten, Jan van, ed. with Dominic Baker-Smith and A. F. Kinney. *Sir Philip Sidney: 1586 and the Creation of a Legend.* Leiden: The Sir Thomas Browne Institute, 1986.

Duhamel, P. Albert, "Sidney's *Arcadia* and Elizabethan Rhetoric." *Studies in Philology* 45 (1948): 134–50.

Duncan-Jones, K. "Sidney's Urania." *Review of English Studies* 17 (1966): 123–32.

Eliot, T. S. *The Use of Poetry and the Use of Criticism.* London: Faber, 1933.

Evans, Maurice, "Divided Aims in the Revised *Arcadia.*" In *Sir Philip Sidney and the Interpretation of Renaissance Culture,* edited by G. F. Waller and M. D. Moore, 1984: 34–43.

Elton, W. R. *"King Lear" and the Gods.* San Marino, Calif.: Huntington Library Publication, 1966.

Freeman, V. C. *Disguise Plots in Elizabethan Drama.* New York: Columbia University Studies in English and Comparative Literature, 1915.

Greenfield, Thelma N. *The Eye of Judgment.* London: Associated University Presses, 1982.

Greville, Fulke. *Poems and Dramas.* Edited by Geoffrey Bullough. Edinburgh and London: 1939. 2 vols.

———. *Prose Works.* Edited by John Gouws. Oxford: Clarendon Press, 1986.

Hamilton, A. C., "Sidney's *Arcadia* as Prose Fiction: Its Relation to Its Sources." *English Literary Renaissance* 2 (1972): 29–60.

Herbert, Edward. *Life.* Edited by J. M. Shuttleworth. London: Oxford University Press, 1976.

Hobsbaum, Philip, ed. *Ten Elizabethan Poets.* London: Longmans, 1969.

Kay, Dennis, ed. *Sir Philip Sidney: An Anthology of Modern Criticism.* Oxford: Clarendon Press, 1987.

King, W. N., "John Lyly and Elizabethan Rhetoric." *Studies in Philology* 52 (1955): 141–61.

Kinney, A. F., "Sidney's Journey to Flushing and Zutphen" in *Sir Philip Sidney: 1586 and the Creation of a Legend,* ed. van Dorsten, Baker-Smith and Kinney.

Lawry, J. S. *Sidney's Two "Arcadias": Pattern and Proceeding.* Ithaca and London: Cornell University Press, 1972.

Leach, C., ed. *Two Gentlemen of Verona.* New Arden, London: Methuen, 1961.

Lewis, C. S. *English Literature in the Sixteenth Century (excluding Drama).* Oxford: Clarendon Press, 1954.

Lindheim, Nancy R., "Sidney's *Arcadia* Book II: Retrospective Narrative." *Studies in Philology* 64 (1967): 159–86.

———. *The Structures of Sidney's "Arcadia."* Toronto and London: University of Toronto Press, 1982.

Lucie-Smith, E., ed. *Penguin Book of Elizabethan Verse.* Harmondsworth: Penguin, 1965.

Lyly, John. *Complete Works.* Edited by R. W. Bond. Oxford: Clarendon Press, 1902. 2 vols.

McCoy, R. C. *Sir Philip Sidney: Rebellion in Arcadia.* Brighton: Harvester Press, 1979.

Marenco, F. *Arcadia Puritana.* Bari: Adriatica Editrice, 1968.

———. "Double Plot in Sidney's *Old Arcadia.*" *Modern Language Review* 64 (1969): 248–63.

———. "Une Apothéose de Genres: Sidney e l'*Arcadia* nella critica letteraria," *Filologia e Letteratura* 12 (1966): 337–76.

McCanles, Michael. "Oracular Prediction and the Fore-Conceit of Sidney's *Arcadia.*" *English Literary History* 50, no. 2 (1983): 233–44.

Milton J. *Eikonoklastes.*

Norbrook, David. *Poetry and Politics in the English Renaissance.* London: Routledge and Kegan Paul: 1984.

O'Connor, John. *"Amadis de Gaule" and Its Influence on Elizabethan Literature.* New Brunswick, N.J.: Rutgers University Press, 1970.

Osborn, James M. *Young Philip Sidney 1572–77.* New Haven and London: Yale University Press, 1972.

Parker, Robert W., "Terentian Structure in Sidney's Original *Arcadia.*" *English Literary Renaissance* 2 (1972): 61–78.

Perkinson, Richard H., "The Epic in Five Acts." *Studies in Philology* 43, 1946: 465–81.

Prescott, A. L. *French Poets and the English Renaissance.* New Haven and London: Yale University Press, 1978.

Rees, Joan. *Samuel Daniel: A Critical and Biographical Study.* Liverpool: Liverpool University Press, 1964.

———. *Fulke Greville, Lord Brooke, 1554–1628.* London: Routledge and Kegan Paul, 1971.

———. Reviews in *Cahiers Elizabéthains*, October 1986: 107–8; and October 1989: 119–20.

———. "Justice, Mercy and a Shipwreck in *Arcadia.*" *Studies in Philology* 87, no. 1 (1990): 75–82.

Roberts, Josephine A. *Architectonic Knowledge in the "New Arcadia" (1590): Sidney's Use of the Heroic Journey.* Salzburg Studies in English Literature 69, 1978.

Rose, Mark, "Sidney's Womanish Man." *Review of English Studies* 15 (1964): 353–63.

Salingar, Leo. *Shakespeare and the Tradition of Comedy.* London: Cambridge University Press, 1974.

Schleiner, Winifred, "Differences of Theme and Structure of the Erona Episode in the *Old* and *New Arcadia.*" *Studies in Philology* 70 (1973): 377–91.

Shakespeare, W. *Alls Well that Ends Well.*

———. *Cymbeline.*

———. *King Lear.*

———. *Othello.*

———. *Richard III.*

————. *The Winters Tale.*

————. *Two Gentlemen of Verona.*

Sinfield, Alan. "Sidney and du Bartas." *Comparative Literature* 27 Winter (1975): 8–20.

————. "Astrophil's Self-Deception." *Essays in Criticism* 28 (1978): 1–18.

————. "Sidney, du Plessis Mornay and the Pagans." *Philological Quarterly* 58 (1979): 26–39.

Skretkowicz, Victor. "Sidney and Amyot: Heliodorus in *New Arcadia.*" *Review of English Studies* 27 (1976): 170–74.

Smith, A. J. *The Metaphysics of Love.* Cambridge: Cambridge University Press, 1985.

Smith, Rowland, ed. *The Greek Romances of Heliodorus, Longus and Achilles Tatius.* London: Bohun's Libraries, 1901.

Spenser, E. *Poetical Works.* Edited by E. de Selincourt. London: Oxford University Press, 1929.

Stone, Lawrence. *The Crisis of the Aristocracy 1558–1641.* London: Oxford University Press, 1967.

Turner, Myron, "The Disfigured Face of Nature: Image and Metaphor in the Revised *Arcadia.*" *English Literary Renaissance* 2 (1972): 116–35.

Vickers, Brian. "A Wrong-Headed Re-write." *Times Literary Supplement* (November 1988): 18–24, 1285.

Walker, D. P. "Ways of Dealing with Atheists," *Bibliothèque d'Humanisme et Renaissance* 17 (1955): 252–77; also in Chapter 4 of *The Ancient Theology,* London: Duckworth, 1972.

Waller, Gary F., ed., with Michael D. Moore. *Sir Philip Sidney and the Interpretation of Renaissance Culture.* London and Sydney: Croom Helm; Totowa, N.J.: Barnes and Noble Books, 1984.

Watson, George. *The English Petrarchans.* London: Warburg Institute Surveys no. 3, 1967.

Weiner, Andrew. *Sir Philip Sidney and the Poetics of Protestantism: A Study of Contexts.* Minneapolis: University of Minnesota, 1978.

White, R. S., "Metamorphosis by Love in Elizabethan Romance, Romantic Comedy and Shakespeare's Early Comedies." *Review of English Studies* 35 (1984): 14–44.

Whitfield, J. H. *A Short History of Italian Literature.* Harmondsworth: Penguin, 1960.

Wolff, S. L. *Greek Romances in Elizabethan Fiction.* New York: *Columbia University Studies in Comparative Literature,* 1912.

Index

Notes are indexed only when they contain matter of substance additional to that in the text.